Michigan Family Field Trips

Michigan Family Field Trips

Fun Sites for Kids

Ellyce Field

The University of Michigan Press
Ann Arbor

Copyright © by Ellyce Field 2008
All rights reserved
Published in the United States of America by
The University of Michigan Press
Manufactured in Singapore
♾ Printed on acid-free paper

2012   2011   2010   2009   5   4   3   2

A CIP catalog record for this book is available from the British Library.

Library of Congress Cataloging-in-Publication Data

Field, Ellyce, 1951–
    Michigan family field trips : fun sites for kids / Ellyce Field.
       p.   cm.
    Includes indexes.
    ISBN-13: 978-0-472-03271-6 (pbk. : alk. paper)
    ISBN-10: 0-472-03271-2 (pbk. : alk. paper)
    1. Michigan—Guidebooks.   2. Family recreation—Michigan—Guidebooks.
3. Children—Travel—Michigan—Guidebooks.   I. Title.

F564.3.F55   2008
977.4—dc22   2007035403

Illustrations and cover art by Andrea Yakima.

To my husband, Steve,
my best friend and travel companion,
for his love and support;
to our grandson, Logan,
who is too little to realize that I wrote this book for him;
and to all future Michigan travelers

Michigan Family Field Trips was written with you in mind—busy parents or grandparents who would like to explore Michigan with your kids or grandkids. I decided to write a book that offers the best Michigan sites for children and to make the book small enough for you to stow in a purse, diaper bag, or car glove box. I visited all of the 60 sites included in this book and also every recommended restaurant—sometimes alone and sometimes with my trusty travel partner and husband, Steve. After a decade writing the Detroit Kids Catalog series with the Wayne State University Press and 20 years writing a weekly family entertainment column in the *Detroit News,* I was very familiar with all of the sites.

It's important to take lots of day trips with your kids. Exploring Michigan and becoming hometown tourists builds a solid base of family experiences and memories, not to mention a large collection of photos. It's always easier if you have your stroller and "go bag" ready with extra diapers, clothes, sweatshirts, caps, sunscreen, snacks, and water. When my kids were small, I also used to keep toys, books, pads of paper, and colored pencils in the car. Then I wouldn't have to frantically look for things right before a trip.

It's also much easier if you become a member of the site you most like to visit. Family memberships run approximately $60–$90 and make great birthday, anniversary, or holiday gifts. They enable you to make shorter visits and come back time and time again. Memberships at science centers, art museums, and zoos are often reciprocal around Michigan. As a member, you'll also receive the site's newsletter, be eligible for discounts in the site's gift shop, and know you're supporting an institution you love to visit.

For this book, I divided Michigan into four sections—Southeastern Michigan, Mid-Michigan, Western Michigan, and Northern Michigan and the Upper Peninsula. Each site description is two pages and includes the following sections: Go Box (basic information), Fun Food (restaurant suggestions), Field Tip (other sites to visit in the general area or special events at the site), and My Notes (space where you can make notes after visiting the site). The information in the Go Box is meant to help you organize your time and look up the site and a map on the Internet. It includes the site's mailing address, phone number and Web address, hours, admission, parking information, and age guidelines. The restaurants I recommend for each site are mostly family-run rather than chains or fast-food. Pretty much every restaurant has a kids' menu. Many also have crayons and encourage kids to color a kids' menu or the restaurant's paper tablecloths. All sites and restaurants listed were chosen by the author (no one paid to be included in this book).

Every effort was made to be sure all the information was correct when this book went to press. However, such travel information as hours, prices, and even locations changes from time to time, so please call ahead. The safety of you and your children is important, so be aware of your surroundings at all times.

I hope you enjoy traveling around Michigan with your kids or grandkids!

Ellyce Field

CONTENTS

Southeastern Michigan

Go Box

220 East Ann Street
Ann Arbor 48104

734-995-5439. www.aahom.org

10–5 Mon.–Sat., noon–5 Sun.

$8 ages 2 & up, free for children under 2

Bring quarters and park in Ann Arbor Police lot on Fifth Ave. or use nearby parking structure on Fourth Ave. & Washington St.

2 & up

My Notes

Fun Food

Kids can order muffins and yogurt sundaes at Afternoon Delight (251 East Liberty St., 734-665-7513), an upscale cafeteria open for breakfast and lunch. Or they can eat at Zingerman's Deli (422 Detroit St., 734-663-3354), where made-to-order was never so exciting. Friendly staff are happy to let you taste olives, meat, and cheese. Take home a loaf of chocolate-cherry bread, my kids' favorite.

Field Tip

Wild Swan Theater, a unique children's theater, offers original plays, often based on children's stories, using masks, mime, puppetry, music, colorful costumes, and continuous American Sign Language interpretation. They also offer behind-the-scenes tours and provide audio-description guides for those who are blind. Plays are performed at Towsley Auditorium, Washtenaw Community College, 4800 E. Huron Dr., Ann Arbor Twp. 48105. For a Wild Swan schedule, call 734-995-0530.

Go Blue! Cheer on your U of M teams. For tickets to sporting events, call the University of Michigan Athletic Office, 734-764-0247.

Dinosaur lovers and mini-paleontologists should check out the University of Michigan Exhibit Museum, 1109 Geddes Ave. On campus, at the corner of North University and Geddes, the museum offers many dinosaur and mastodon skeletons and bones, plus static exhibits of wildlife, Michigan geography, and Native American life. The planetarium (734-764-0478) offers changing shows about the seasonal sky and weather.

The Ann Arbor Hands-On Museum is a giant four-level playground where kids explore and become young scientists. In the Preschool Gallery, a huge self-contained room, toddlers wear firemen's hats and climb on a red fire truck; sit at kid-sized tables to look at leaves and insects; play with pots, pans, and plastic food in a small climbing house; and tumble around a play area full of colorful, cushioned blocks. Best of all, at the water tables, toddlers put on aprons, belly up to the troughs, and play with water toys—plastic sharks, boats, and gears. When they are finished, there are dryers to dry off hands and clothes. (Older children will appreciate their own water tables across the hall from the Preschool Gallery.)

The museum has other kid-pleasers. On the second floor, older children climb on the climbing wall, while all ages play music on gigantic piano keys, fool around at sand and bubble tables, and become surrounded by a giant soaplike bubble in the bubble capsule. The Discovery Room is perfect for budding paleontologists. It's full of shells, skeletons, rocks and skulls, magnifying glasses, and discovery books.

The third and fourth floors are very small and should remind you of their original use as the upper level of a firehouse. You'll find a light harp and shadow wall on the third level. The fourth level lets kids build geometric shapes and become television hosts.

In addition to traveling exhibits, the museum offers special family days during school vacations, with such engaging workshops as making and eating ice cream.

The well-stocked gift shop has robot, dinosaur, and slime kits; plush toys, kaleidoscopes, costumes, puzzles, books, telescopes, rocks, and crystals; and a lot of inexpensive toys that would make great party favors. The museum offers birthday parties, camps, and scout badge workshops.

Go Box

13624 Michigan Avenue
Dearborn 48126

313-582-2266. www.theaanm.org

10–6 Wed., Fri., & Sat.,
10–8 Thurs., noon–5 Sun.

$6 adults, $3 ages 6–12 & seniors,
free for children 5 & under

Free in the lot behind the museum

4 & up

My Notes

Fun Food

At Al-Ameer's (12170 W. Warren, 313-582-8185), kids enjoy the colorful murals and Mideastern foods—falafel, shish kebab, fatoush salad, chicken shawarma, and specialty juice smoothies. For upscale Arabic and French pastries and Kashta ice cream (which tastes a little like fragrant gelato), be sure to end your visit at Shatilla Bakery (14300 W. Warren, 313-582-1952). Order at the counter and take some treats home, but enjoy part of your snack in the center of the bakery, surrounded by twinkling lights and palm trees.

Field Tip

The gift shop is a virtual bazaar representing wares from all over the Arab world. Kids will find dolls, stuffed animals, T-shirts, candy, Arabic children's books, music, and jewelry. The museum offers tours and workshops. At 2–4 on Sundays, Target sponsors free craft workshops for children.

Arab American National Museum

This new museum is for families who value diversity and those with Arabic backgrounds who would like to share their culture with their children. Located across the street from the Dearborn City Hall, the airy museum's three levels tell a story of the many cultures, lands, and people who historically and currently make up the Arab world.

Start by listening carefully in the mosaic-tiled and domed atrium. Hear trickling water from the center fountain and haunting music. Glass cases holding historic artifacts ring the room and introduce kids to the arts and architecture of the historic Arab world and the three religions—Christianity, Judaism, and Islam—that make up monotheism. Kids enjoy pressing buttons and hearing the sounds of a *takht*—a small Arabic musical ensemble including a *tablah* (handheld drum), *riqq* (tambourine), *nay* (flute), *ud* (stringed instrument), *quanun* (zither), and violin.

As you walk up the grand staircase to the second floor, there's a huge map of the current Arab world and a slide show of the many faces of Arabic people. The second floor's two large galleries contain artifacts—many static and some participatory—explaining when, how, and from where Arabs came to the United States. Arab Americans can trace their own roots and find Syrian, Lebanese, Chaldean, Palestinian, or Egyptian stories, among others.

On the third floor, learn about famous Arab Americans in every walk of life, like astronaut/teacher Christa McAuliffe, heart surgeon Dr. Michael DeBakey, political activist Ralph Nader, and race car driver Bobby Rahal.

5

Go Box

315 East Warren Avenue
Detroit 48201

313-494-5800. www.maah-detroit.org

9–3 Tues.–Thurs., 9–5 Fri. &
Sat., 1–5 Sun.

$8 ages 13 & up, $5 ages 3–12 &
seniors, free for children under 3

Free on site

5 & up

My Notes

Fun Food

Drive two miles east to Eastern Market (2934 Russell St., 313-833-1560) and park in the main lot. If you go on a Saturday in summer, expect lots of traffic and congestion. Bring your stroller or wagon to pull the kids through the outdoor farmers' stalls and load up on fresh fruits and vegetables. Other times during the year are quiet. There are several good restaurants for lunch. My favorite is the Russell Street Deli (2465 Russell St., 313-567-2900), a noisy, unadorned restaurant with large sandwiches.

Field Tip

The museum offers Black History Month events during February, sponsors the African World Festival at Hart Plaza in August, and has a family day for Kwanzaa in December. School and community groups can also schedule workshops and tours.

To learn more about Berry Gordy Jr. and the Motown Sound, take a tour of the nearby Motown Historical Museum (2648 West Grand Blvd., Detroit 48208; 313-875-2264).

This beautiful gold-domed building is the largest African American History museum in the country. Its new core exhibit is a wonderfully evocative high-tech, animated journey from an African village to Detroit in the 20th century. For schoolchildren, it makes history come to life.

Walk slowly through the two-level space, with its 22 galleries, life-sized casts, interactive kiosks, time lines, and simulated historical scenes. You come face-to-face with an African marketplace, the horrors of a slave dungeon and slave ship, a slave auction block, and a Southern plantation. You learn about the Underground Railroad from talking mannequins of Harriet Tubman and Frederick Douglass.

You learn about the Great Migration through a simulation of the Ford Rouge foundry, see a street in Black Bottom, and step into the Paradise Theatre to watch short film clips by African Americans. You learn about the sports and labor histories of the city from eavesdropping near a barbershop and then meet barrier-breaking doctors—including Charles H. Wright, who started the museum. Walk into a church and learn about Detroit's role during the civil rights movement, watch the 1967 riots on a television screen, hear the Motown sound, and, finally, at the end of the journey, meet a life-size cast of Detroit's first black mayor, Coleman A. Young.

Go Box

201 North Street
Chelsea 48118

734-475-1361. www.jiffymix.com

Tours of approximately 1½ hours for up to 45 people scheduled 9–1:30 Mon.–Fri. Call ahead to schedule tour.

Free

Free on site

Must be at least 6 years old to tour plant (younger children can remain in the tour center with an adult while group tours the plant)

My Notes

Fun Food

Eat lunch at The Common Grill (112 S. Main St., 734-475-0470), the most famous restaurant in town, upscale and always consistently good. Satisfy your sweet tooth with chocolates and chocolate drinks at Gourmet Chocolates (312 N. Main St., 734-475-1071); there's even a children's play area where kids can read, play in a little kitchen, and ride a rocking horse.

Field Tip

If your kids like teddy bears, stop at Chelsea Teddy Bear Co. (310 N. Main Street), across the street from the milling company. In this huge retail outlet, you'll find bears of all sizes, shapes, and colors, as well as their clothes. Tours of the glassed-in factory area are at 11, 1, and 3 on Saturdays or may be scheduled. The outlet also holds birthday parties and workshops. For tour reservations, call 734-433-5499 or visit www.chelseateddybearcompany.com.

The Chelsea Milling Co.'s Jiffy Mix Tour is good, old-fashioned fun. Ushered by a friendly guide into the small auditorium, you watch the history of the milling company and all of its special Jiffy mixes in a slide show on a screen pulled down from the ceiling, with a tour guide with a bullhorn enunciating the audio portion. Next you have your choice of hot or cold drinks and at least three different tasty Jiffy Mix snacks at tables set up in the reception room, which is wood-paneled like a 1950s den.

You then put on your hairnet and file out of the den, up the stairs, and into the plant, which hasn't changed much in its 75-plus years. It's clean and airy and smells like raspberry chocolate. Your tour guide continues to point out parts of the factory, shouting through the bullhorn. Actual workers glide past you; the floor vibrates under you; conveyer belts near you and above your head slowly and methodically fill boxes with mix, close them, put on their labels, and pack them. The little boxes sashay along their path, and everyone from tour goer to employee is smiling and happy. After the tour, take home several boxes as freebies. More boxes are available for purchase.

Go Box

2100 Woodward Avenue
Detroit 48201

Single games, 866-66-TIGER [668-4437];
season & group tickets, 313-471-BALL
[2255]

Apr.–Oct.: usually 1:05 & 7:05

$5–$65

$8–$20 in supervised lots within blocks
of the ballpark

All ages

My Notes

Fun Food

The Big Cat Court and concessions throughout the park offer a variety of foods, from Little Caesar's pizza and hot dogs to salads and fries. Across the street, in Foxtown, is Johnny Rockets (2239 Woodward, 313-471-3446), a 1950s diner with hamburgers and milk shakes. Take Red Wing fans and out-of-towners to Hockeytown Café (2301 Woodward, 313-965-9500).

Field Tip

Kids 14 and under can become Tigers Kids Club members and be privy to lots of Tigers freebies and perks, including an official badge with lanyard, two complimentary passes for upper box seats for a game, player posters, a Detroit Tigers sticker sheet, a magnet, newsletters, and the opportunity to go to the front of the line to run the bases on Sundays. Sign up online or call 313-471-2224.

Tours of Comerica Park for groups of 15 or more are available on nongame Tuesdays and Fridays, June–September, at 10, noon, and 2. Call 313-471-2074.

For small children, enjoying a baseball game requires food and team paraphernalia and a funny mascot. The Detroit Tigers have all that and more. At Comerica Park—part theme park, part stadium—kids have fun whether or not the team wins, which is something the Tigers front office cemented in the dreary years before the team became a World Series contender.

Ride a hand-painted tiger or a chariot on the Big Cat Court's carousel, or ride a baseball 50 feet into the air on the Brushfire Grill's Ferris wheel. Paws, the team mascot, his behind bobbing to the music, is always up for a photo and a hug.

On Kids Day, every Sunday during the season, face painters are on hand, children 14 and under ride the Ferris wheel and the carousel for free, and after the game kids can run the bases. There's a mammoth water fountain in center field that spouts colorful water whenever the Tigers hit a home run and after the Friday and Saturday evening games there are fireworks.

Regale your kids with Tigers lore by looking at the six larger-than-life sculptures along the left center field wall. They include Ty Cobb, Charlie Gehringer, Hank Greenberg, Willie Horton, Al Kaline, and Hal Newhouser.

Arrive early and show the kids the outside of Comerica Park, where orange and blue Pewabic tiles share the decor with mounted tiger faces who've caught baseballs in their mouths. Take a picture of the kids next to the giant tiger at the Gate A entrance.

Best of all, teach your kids that summer means wearing your sunscreen and Tigers caps, sitting in the stands, eating a hot dog, and cheering for the home team.

Go Box

39221 Woodward Avenue
Bloomfield Hills 48304

248-645-3320 or 248-645-3323.
www.cranbrookart.edu/museum

11–5 Wed.–Sun., 11–9 fourth Fri.
of each month

$6 adults, $4 seniors & students,
free for children 12 & under

Free parking in lot east of museum &
around semicircle in front of museum

4 & up

My Notes

Fun Food

Drive south on Woodward into Birmingham, under 10 minutes away, and
you'll find lots of restaurants. Kids do well at Leo's Coney Island (154 S.
Woodward, 248-540-8780).

Field Tip

If you are artsy or encourage the arts, you'll want to take your children to
the museum's family days, great afternoons of unusual art projects.

Cranbrook Art Museum

Cranbrook Art Museum features arts and crafts items from the Cranbrook Collection and famous modern art from its newer collection, plus small traveling shows. It's intimate and cozy, with two floors of small galleries, often a video pertaining to an exhibition, and a great gift shop. Connected to the Cranbrook Art Academy, where students can receive an MFA, the museum is also a showcase of the avant-garde and witty during twice-a-year student shows. Surprising, colorful, and amusing pieces of art offer children a wonderful first-time art experience.

Visit in good weather and be rewarded by the vista to the south, outside the museum's door. Eliel Saarinen, the academy's first president and architect of the Cranbrook community, laid out a symmetrical walkway of reflecting pools and landscape. Explore the outdoor sculpture on all sides of the museum. My children enjoyed seeing the Orpheus Fountain, which they thought were "people taking a shower."

Go Box

39221 Woodward Avenue
Bloomfield Hills 48304

248-645-3200; group tours,
248-645-3210. science.cranbrook.edu

10–5 daily, 10–10 Fri.

$8 adults, $6 ages 2–12 & seniors, free for children under 2. Bat Zone, $4 plus museum admission. Laser & astronomy programs, $3 plus museum admission.

Free on site

2 & up

My Notes

Fun Food

Take hungry mini-scientists to the Reflections Café, the museum's upscale coffee shop, where you'll also find sandwiches, soups, pizza, and snacks.

Field Tip

The Bat Zone, in a separate small building behind the main museum, is the home of more than 90 bats, all rescued and hanging upside down in large cages. Walk into their warm and semi-darkened world and learn how they help the environment (they eat thousands of mosquitoes, for one thing) and aren't the scary predators of popular culture (these bats are all fruit-eating). Friendly handlers from the Organization for Bat Conservation put on public shows daily Memorial Day–Labor Day and at 1:30, 2:30, and 3:30 Sat. & Sun. the rest of the year. The Bat Zone is sometimes also home to an injured sloth or flying squirrels.

Cranbrook Institute of Science

A visit to Cranbrook Institute of Science has always been a way to reinforce science for school-age children. Under one roof, you'll find a life-sized *T. rex* skeleton, a gigantic furry mastodon, lots of stuffed birds, a slice of a giant redwood tree, a huge rock collection, dinosaur bones, botany specimens, evolution dioramas, weather games, physics gears, and a beautiful new audio about Native Americans. There are buttons to push and even a dome to enter to see an audiovisual presentation on how birds are related to dinosaurs. Kids enjoy the Motion Room, with its gears and Rube Goldberg contraption; the Observatory, where, on a clear night, you can look through the telescope and see Saturn; and the Weather Station, where you can stand in the middle of a rainstorm. There is even a science play area for toddlers, complete with books, puzzles, and a Little Tykes computer.

Catch an astronomy or musical laser show in the planetarium. Children three and under might find the absolute darkness frightening. Buy your tickets ahead or when you first enter. Shows are offered Saturday and Sunday year-round and daily during the summer and school holidays.

The excitement is ratcheted up three times a year when the museum hosts a hands-on traveling exhibit that teaches kids through fooling around, touching, and having fun. The museum offers classes, workshops, field trips, birthday parties, and seasonal events, such as the Maple Syrup Festival in March, the Bat Fest in August, Chemistry Day and Halloween Science in October, and special daily activities during Thanksgiving weekend and December school break.

This is one gift shop where you'll want to set each child's monetary limit before you enter. It has an incredible amount of science-related toys, games, books, plush toys, kits, and even insect-laden candy.

Go Box

5401 Woodward Avenue
Detroit 48202

313-833-1805.
www.detroithistorical.org

9:30–3 Wed.–Fri., 10–5 Sat.,
noon–5 Sun.

$6 adults, $4 students,
free for children under 4

$3 in lot on Kirby,
west of museum

4 & up

My Notes

Fun Food

Walk west two short blocks along Kirby into the Wayne State Campus for Jimmy Johns, Starbucks, and Einstein Bagels, all waiting for you on Anthony Wayne Dr. Or drive south along Woodward less than a mile to Union Street Saloon (4145 Woodward, 313-831-3965) for salads, soups, and sandwiches.

Field Tip

Be sure to come back to the museum for special events highlighting Detroit history and featuring crafts, snacks, and live entertainment. These include African American Family Day in February, Detroit's Birthday Party in July, and Treats in the Streets in October.

For multicultural programs, craft projects, and intimate Starlab planetarium shows, head over to the Detroit Children's Museum (6134 Second Ave., 313-873-8100, www.detroitchildrensmuseum.org).

The Mosaic Youth Theatre is also nearby. For a schedule of their award-winning season of public and school performances, call 313-872-6910 or visit www.mosaicdetroit .org.

Take a spin on the brand-new River Carousel, whose 19 colorful animal figures are based on Detroit River wildlife. The carousel is located in the new Rivard Plaza at the foot of Rivard and the RiverWalk, the new 3.5-mile-long walkway alongside the Detroit River, between Renaissance Center and Belle Isle. The carousel is open during spring, summer, and fall. Rides are $2.

Parents and grandparents who grew up in Detroit know all about this museum's spooky Streets of Old Detroit. Located in the museum's lower level, the streets are just as wonderful as you remember them. Walk along cobblestones and then bricks as you go through Detroit in the 1840s, 1870s, and 1900s. Kids can peek into the storefront windows of drug, toy, and shoe stores and see old-fashioned merchandise. Three sites have talking mannequins, which make the era come alive. In the blacksmith shop, overhear a conversation about the Underground Railroad; in the bank, a widow applies for a loan after her husband has died in a cholera epidemic; in the fire station, horses neigh, and firemen get ready for action.

Adjacent to the Streets is Glancy Toy Trains, four levels of an expansive collection of moving trains amid city and country buildings, bridges, a circus, a Wild West show, and much more. Kids can press buttons to hear stories or music and can see close-ups on video screens.

There are two major exhibits on the main level of the museum, From Frontier to Factories and Motor City. Both reward patient children with a look at the history of Detroit through hands-on displays, walk-into exhibits, and video screens. Kids press buttons to hear specific stories of the past, told through the eyes of people representing Detroit's diverse population. Learn how Detroit went from fur trading post to stove capital to motor city. Walk along the catwalk of the old Chrysler plant and look over the car factory displays. On the museum's top floor, you'll find changing exhibits featuring pop culture or fashion.

The gift shop is a great place to find history-based toys, games, and activity books. You'll also find snacks, miniature cars, posters, books, and puppets.

Go Box

5200 Woodward Avenue
Detroit 48202

313-833-7900; box office, 313-833-4005;
school tours, 313-833-7981. www.dia.org

10–5 Wed. & Thurs., 10–10 Fri.,
10–6 Sat. & Sun.

$8 adults, $5 children, $6 seniors.
Audio tour $2 extra

$6 valet parking at Woodward entrance;
or use lot on John R (east of museum),
metered street parking, or underground
parking on Farnsworth

All ages

My Notes

Fun Food

You can find something for everyone at the CaféDIA, an upscale cafeteria serving hot and cold entrées, sandwiches, salads, soups, desserts, and drinks. Or have a snack and drink at the Kresge Court Coffee Shop.

Field Tip

The DIA has worked very hard to become family friendly under its new visitor-friendly mandate. There are art workshops, storytelling, puppet shows, and special family events on weekends; colorful treasure hunt sheets; a youth component on the audio tour; and, best of all, "I Spy" labels hung at child's eye level to help children find items of interest in the galleries. The museum also offers art classes and workshops, day camps, and special holiday events during the summer and December school break.

The Museum of Contemporary Art Detroit (4454 Woodward Avenue, 313-832-6622) offers free family workshops each month in conjunction with their exhibitions.

Detroit Institute of Arts

Take your children to the Detroit Institute of Arts (DIA) at an early age and keep visiting. Soon they'll have their favorite installations and galleries. It might be the inscrutable mummies; the otherworldly African, Oceanic, or South American masks; the cases of splendidly engraved armor; the galleries of colorful and minimal contemporary art; or the aristocratic family meal—a video display in the French Decorative Arts gallery. Be sure to introduce them to Artie the Donkey, the only piece of art in the museum that can be touched (he sits on the second floor in the family area, near the elevator right above the Farnsworth Entrance). Snake down the spooky spiral staircase found in the first gallery on your right off the Great Hall.

Bring a pad of paper and some pencils and let your mini-artists sit on the floor and sketch what they see. Help them really look at a painting or sculpture. Have them mimic the painted subject's pose, gesture, or facial expression.

Since the DIA is so huge—30 percent more gallery space was added during renovations completed in November 2007—only stay for a short time with your children. Have a snack or a meal, buy something in the gift shop, and leave with them wanting more. The gift shop has a huge inventory of art-oriented children's books, kits, games, puzzles, plush toys, and puppets.

Go Box

25 East Grand River Avenue
Detroit 48226

313-961-7777.
www.puppetart.org

Public shows at 2 on Sat.; puppetry workshops offered after the show. Group shows & workshops during the week. PuppetART also travels to sites.

$7 adults, $5 children. Puppetry workshop, $8. Call for group & travel fees.

Metered street parking, or use nearby lots

3 & up

My Notes

Fun Food

Walk over to Campus Martius Park and order sandwiches, soup, salads, and cookies at Au Bon Pain (800 Woodward, 313-226-6600). Or treat the kids to Detroit's own Hard Rock Café (in the Compuware Building, 45 Monroe St., 313-964-7625), also within walking distance.

Field Tip

During the summer, Campus Martius features movies; you can rent ice skates and skate on the pond during the winter. Enjoy early February's annual Detroit's Winter Blast, held along Woodward from downtown to Campus Martius, featuring a big ice slide and other outdoor winter games.

To see giant papier-mâché puppet-type heads, tour the Parade Company (9500 Mt. Elliott, Studio A), responsible for America's Thanksgiving Parade. To schedule a tour, call 313-923-7400 or visit www.theparade.org.

Detroit Puppet Theater

PuppetART is the creative endeavor of three Russian émigrés, all formally trained in Russian theater arts and puppetry. The troupe offers a monthly repertoire of puppet shows in their cozy Detroit Puppet Theater. Each puppet show is an international folktale or original story performed in a sophisticated manner using music, dialogue, and beautifully dressed handmade marionettes and other puppet forms. Adults will realize that puppet shows are perfect for them, too.

In the last ten years, Detroit Puppet Theater has grown. The intimate theater with its puppet stage and tiered seating is just one part of the whole puppetry experience. Now there's a museum of puppets from around the world, including Japan, Russia, Sicily, Czechoslovakia, and Yoruba, Africa. On display are also many of the puppets created for PuppetART shows and, on loan, a collection of Meredith Bixby's famous puppets.

The front room houses a gift shop with snacks, drinks, and inexpensive puppets and puppet paraphernalia. It also functions as a birthday party room or workshop area, perfect for staying after a puppet show to create your own puppet, celebrating a child's birthday, or bringing in a scout troop for a puppet workshop.

PuppetART offers a repertoire of eight puppet shows, performed on Saturdays, September–May. These include "The Firebird," "Close the Window," "Crane Maiden," "Oh, Ananse!" "Turtle Island," "Book of Esther," "Kolobok," and "Banana for Turtle." Three annual festivals in February (African Folklore), April (Puppetry Month), and December (Holiday Month) may feature guest puppeteers or special programming.

Go Box

5020 John R Street
Detroit 48202

313-577-8400.
www.detroitsciencecenter.org

Summer: 9–5 Mon.–Fri., 10:30–6 Sat.,
noon–6 Sun. Winter, 9–3 Mon–Fri.,
10:30–6 Sat., noon–6 Sun. Extended hours
during school breaks & special exhibits.

$7.95 adults, $6.95 children & seniors.
Combo prices are $4 for first theater, dis-
counted for second theater. Special fee for
traveling show.

$6 in lot on John R adjacent to entrance

2 & up

My Notes

Fun Food

Take a break with your mini-scientists and eat at the museum's
Science Café, where they sell sandwiches, salads, soups, and
snacks. Or, if you're finished fooling around with science, drive
four miles west to Mexican Town and treat the kids to authentic
Mexican food and large portions at Xochimilco (3409 Bagley
Street, Detroit 48216; 313-843-0179) or Evie's Tamales (3454
Bagley, 313-843-5056).

Field Tip

The Detroit Science Center's gift shop is a treasure chest of science toys, kits, and books; telescopes, plush toys, T-shirts, and
gifts representing traveling exhibits. Kids will even find inexpensive pencils, erasers, rubber animals, and dinosaurs, priced just
right for their allowance.

Detroit Science Center

The Detroit Science Center's three floors of exhibits, shows, and demonstrations are airy, colorful, and spacious. There's so much going on at one time, it's important to plan your visit, because what you do and see depends greatly on the age of your children.

Check out the times of the IMAX Dome Theatre's movies and the planetarium's shows, and buy your tickets when you first come in. As the lights go down in the 360-degree domed theater, a huge movie wraps around you in sight, sound, and movement. Soar to the top of a snowcapped mountain, swim with a school of fish in the ocean depths, kayak down the crashing Nile, or walk weightless on the moon. The movement and darkness might be too upsetting for children three and under, but older children will want to experience more. In the technologically updated Dassault Systemes Planetarium, kids dramatically learn about the night sky or the universe on a wide, three-story-high dome with surround sound.

If you are visiting with preschoolers, make a beeline for the SBC Children's Gallery, where kids can explore dinosaurs, play with water and real plants, crawl through honeycomb cells, look at bugs under microscopes, curl up with science books, make a simple science project, dress up, and pretend with puppets. All ages enjoy the silliness and wonderment of the electrifying DTE Energy Sparks Theater and the audience-participatory Chrysler Science Stage. Older kids can wander through a rain forest and become amazed by the cascading two-story interactive waterfall, learn about heart health and the marvels of manufacturing, play with gizmos and levers, create tornadoes, make a hot air balloon rise, refract light, and hear sound from a laser harp.

At least two times a year, the museum features not-to-be-missed traveling exhibits. It also offers birthday parties, special family workshops, summer camps, and, for grades K–12, group tours, workshops, and traveling science shows.

23

Go Box

8540 West Ten Mile Road
Royal Oak 48067

248-541-5717; 24-hour information,
248-398-0900. www.detroitzoo.org

Apr.–Oct.: 10–5 daily, 10–8 Wed. during July
& Aug. Nov.–Mar.: 10–4 daily.

$11 ages 13–61, $7 ages 2–12, $9 seniors,
free for children under 2. Mini-train, daily
May–Sept., weekends only in Oct., $2 one-
way, free for under 2. Wild Simulator Ride,
$4. Strollers, wagons, & wheelchairs available
for rental.

$5 in lots adjacent to entrance

All ages

My Notes

Fun Food

During the summer, concessions located throughout the park sell soft drinks, water, ice cream, hamburgers, hot dogs, garden burgers, pizza, chicken tenders, and other snacks. During the winter, only the Arctic Food Court is open, selling soup, among other things. Bring a picnic and eat in the three-acre, 40-table main picnic grove behind the Wildlife Interpretive Gallery. Or go into downtown Royal Oak to Comet Burgers (207 S. Main Street, 248-414-4567) and introduce the kids to a 1950s diner complete with juke box, pink vinyl stools, and a full menu of hamburgers, fries, malts, and Sander's hot fudge sundaes.

Field Tip

The Wild Simulator Ride, located in the Ford Education Center, takes kids at least 36 inches tall and five years or older on a seated motion-simulated thrill ride in a big-screen theater. Four movies are rotated—*Dino Island*, *Dino Island II*, *Wilderness Adventure*, and *Deep Sea*. Check at the entry for movie schedule and times.

Detroit Zoo

At the Detroit Zoo, kids run down floral trimmed paths and bump into outdoor areas of grazing camels or deer, flamingos, and wild horses. They can find lions napping in the sun on a bleached rocky outcrop or tigers sitting in the shade. At the Australian Outback Adventure, kids walk through a dusty Australian habitat for an up-close view of kangaroos and the wildlife they live among. At the Arctic Ring of Life, they walk through a clear Plexiglas, water-filled tunnel and come face-to-face with floating sea otters and polar bears diving for food.

They can check out the chimps and gorillas frolicking in trees and grassy areas at the Great Apes of Harambee. At the Wild Life Interpretive Gallery, there's a coral reef aquarium and an attached butterfly garden, where velvety butterflies land on you. At the connected Free Flight Aviary, kids see large nests and exotic birds. They stroll through a rain forest at the National Amphibian Conservation Center and see all sorts of frogs, toads, salamanders, and newts.

That's just the tip of the iceberg, so to speak. There are hundreds of animals behind each twist and turn, in state-of-the-art indoor and outdoor exhibits. There are also a miniature train and colorful and inviting playscapes. You can also feed giraffes at the new Giraffe Encounter.

The zoo offers birthday parties, overnights, summer camps, group outings, and special events, including Wild Winter Weekends in January and February, ethnic festivals and concerts in the summer, Zoo Boo in October, and Breakfast with Santa in December. The main gift shop, near the entrance, is stocked to the gills with animal- and conservation-themed toys, books, plush animals and puppets, lunch bags, back packs, sippy cups, games, puzzles, and clothes.

Go Box

24 Frank Lloyd Wright Drive
Ann Arbor 48106

734-998-0182; group tours,
734-930-3188. www.pettingfarm.com

9:30–4 Mon.–Fri., 10:30–5 Sat. & Sun.
Open year-round, but call to verify
hours during winter months. Call ahead
to schedule tours.

$5 adults, $4.50 ages 2–12 & seniors.
Winter: $2.50/person.

Free on site

Infants–10 years

My Notes

Fun Food

Prolong the pastoral feeling by bringing a picnic and sitting at covered picnic tables. Kids can feed crusts to the ducks in the pond. If you are part of a group, you can order Domino's Pizza ahead: $3.50/person includes two slices of pizza and a beverage.

Field Tip

Have a down-on-the-farm birthday, complete with farmhouse party room (available on Saturdays or Sundays). All packages include a hayride, the petting farm, and a pizza lunch. Pony rides are available at an additional cost. Call the group number to arrange a party.

If your children would like to see lots of cows up close and also tour an ice cream production facility, go to Cook's Farm Dairy (2950 Seymour Lake Road, Ortonville 48462; 248-627-3329).

Domino's Petting Farm

Domino's Petting Farm offers young children a friendly first-time experience on a farm. The barns and adjoining area are clean, the animals docile, and the farmer-guides welcoming. Take a tractor-drawn hayride around 15 acres and watch for the Domino's herd of buffalo. Sit on haystacks in the red barn for an audience participation animal show. You'll learn what to call female and male cows (heifers and bulls), how to feed a baby cow (with a bottle of milk), and all sorts of silly animal facts. After the show, walk slowly through the barn, meeting and petting horses, donkeys, sheep, goats, chicken, rabbits, pigs, and llamas. Depending on the season, you might even see baby animals (most are born in spring and summer). If you visit during the winter, you'll find the barn open to visitors, but no show or hayride.

Domino's Petting Farm holds a huge Easter Egg Hunt for kids ages 1–10, with more than 20,000 eggs, plus hayrides, pony rides, animal demonstrations, and a visit from the Easter Bunny. Proceeds benefit Make-A-Wish Foundation.

Go Box

61475 Silver Lake Road
South Lyon 48178

Information & group tours, 888-824-3377 or
248-437-0150; recorded message, 248-437-
4701. www.erwinorchards.com

U-pick apples: 9–6 daily, mid–Aug. through
Oct. 31 (last wagon leaves for orchard at 5:30).
U-pick pumpkins: 9–6 daily during Oct. Cider
mill/farm market, 6–6 daily, mid-Aug.–early
Nov. U-pick sweet cherries begins July 4. U-pick
red raspberries begins late July. Call ahead to
confirm dates & crop availability.

Free wagon ride to the orchard; pay ahead for
½-bushel or peck bags. Most of the features of
the kiddie play area are free; a few have $1 fee;
25 cents for goat or lamb feed. Fee for
Halloween barns.

Free on site

All ages

My Notes

Fun Food

The farm market sells quarts and half quarts of cider, plus cider slush and
hot cider, caramel apples, hot dogs, nachos, cinnamon doughnuts, and the
Erwin specialty—pumpkin doughnuts with autumn sprinkles. It's fun to
sip on cider and eat doughnuts at a picnic table in the sunny autumn
weather.

Field Tip

Until the developers catch up with them, there are still many farms offering U-pick fruits. The season starts in June with strawberries and runs
through summer cherries and blueberries and fall raspberries, apples,
and pumpkins. For a directory of U-pick farms, visit www.mda.state
.mi.us/market /u-pick/index.asp. Here are my favorites:

Blake's Big Apple Orchard, 71485 North Ave., Armada 48005; 586-784-9710.
Blake's Orchard and Cider Mill, 17985 Armada Center Rd., Armada 48005;
    586-784-5343.
Erie Orchards, 1235 Erie Rd., Erie 48133; 734-848-4518.
Plymouth Orchards and Cider Mill, 10685 Warren Rd., Plymouth 48170;
    734-455-2290.
Spicer Orchards Farm Market and Cider Mill, 10411 Clyde Rd., Fenton 48430;
    810-632-7692.
Uncle John's Cider Mill, 8614 N. U.S. 127, St. Johns 48879; 989-224-3686.
Wiard's Orchards, 5565 Merritt Rd., Ypsilanti 48197; 734-482-7744.

Erwin Orchards

Take the kids to Erwin Orchards, where dwarf apple trees are just the right size. After a five-minute wagon ride (free of prickly hay), children are ready to become farmers for a day. Kids two and older quickly recognize the fun of plucking ripe reddish-green apples from drooping branches and stowing them carefully in a plastic bushel or peck bag. Within 20 minutes, you'll fill your bag and be ready for the bumpy ride back to the farm market and play area. Put the fruit in the car and come into the fragrant farm market. It's time for your annual cider and doughnut fix. You can eat your treats while basking in the sun in the picnic area, then watch the kids as they explore the play area. There's a hay bale maze, caterpillar balloon crawl, and trike trail, plus lambs and goats to pet and feed, a working beehive to watch, and a few cardboard tableaux—featuring Johnny Appleseed and animals—for children to stick their little heads through for a parental photo opportunity. In October, there's a Barn of Horrors for older children and a Children's Spooky Barn for small children, both running noon–5 Saturday and Sunday.

Go Box

20900 Oakwood Boulevard
Dearborn 48124

313-271-1620; groups, 313-982-6001.
www.thehenryford.org

Buses depart from Henry Ford Museum each
half hour, 9:30–2:30, last tour leaving at 2:30.
Plant hours: Jan. 1–mid-Apr. and after Labor
Day–Dec. 31, 9:30–5 Mon.–Sat.; mid-Apr.–
Labor Day, 9:30–5 Mon.–Sun. While the tour
doesn't guarantee you'll see an assembly line in
full operation, the Rouge Tour Web site does list
the days and times trucks aren't being built. It's
more fun to visit during a production time.

$14 adults, $10 ages 5–12, $13 seniors

Free in lot south of Henry Ford Museum

6 & up

Fun Food

Eat at Henry Ford Museum's Michigan Café. Be sure to ask for
the Kid Cruiser. It comes with a choice of PB&J, chicken tenders, or a hot dog, plus cookie and chips, served in (what else?)
a car. (See Henry Ford Museum for more options.)

Field Tip

Be sure to make this an intergenerational outing and tell your
kids about your family's connection to the car industry. Many
men immigrated to Detroit in 1914 and later to cash in on
Ford's offer of work for $5 a day. Your child's own great-great-
grandfather may have been one of those men.

My Notes

Ford Rouge Factory Tour

Bring the kids to the only car tour left in Michigan. The Ford Rouge Tour—part theme park, part real factory tour—sums up Detroit's and Henry Ford's automobile legacies. The fun starts with a 25-minute bus ride. A video on the bus sets the scene and identifies the historic buildings of the Rouge Plant complex.

Then step inside the spacious visitor center, where friendly greeters hustle you into the Legacy Theater for a 12-minute film outlining the history of the Rouge Plant. Learn about Henry Ford's invention of the assembly line, how immigrants flocked to Dearborn to work in his car manufacturing plant for $5 a day, how the labor union formed, and battles they fought at the plant. Next, you're ushered into Theater Two for the highlight of the tour. Buckle your seatbelt and enjoy a multisensory, multiscreen, theater-in-the-round, where you watch a car go from design to test drive. You feel the heat of the blast furnace, see the sparks of the welding machine, are misted with sweet-smelling "spray paint," and feel the floor rumble beneath you as the car takes to the open road.

It just gets better as you walk into the truck plant on a one-third-mile catwalk, high above real people working on real trucks on real assembly lines. You can meander and read some of the kiosks, try the buttons on the computer videos, and learn about truck manufacture today.

From the environmental Observation Deck, get a bird's-eye view of the plant, see its living, green sedem roof, and learn how the plant is becoming environmentally sustainable. The 90-minute tour ends in the Legacy Lobby, where five famous Rouge products are on display—a 1929 Ford Model A Roadster, a 1932 Ford V8 Victoria, a 1949 Ford Club Coupe, a 1956 Thunderbird, and a 1965 Mustang. Hit the gift shop for car paraphernalia, toys, games, kits, and clothes. There are even Ford Factory Tour badges for scouts.

Go Box

Waterford Oaks County Park
1702 Scott Lake Road
Waterford 48328

248-975-4440. www.oakgov.com/parksrec/
ppark/fridge.html

Mid-December–mid-March: 5–9 Mon.–Tues.,
4–9:30 Wed.–Fri., 10–10 Sat., noon–6 Sun.

$2.50 for single ride. All-day passes, $4 children 30–43 inches tall, $7 Oakland County
residents over 43 inches tall, $10 nonresidents.

Free on site

Riders must be at least 30 inches tall. Children
11 & under must be accompanied by an adult.
Mittens or gloves required.

My Notes

Fun Food

Lookout Lodge, located near the base of the Fridge, is a great place to warm up and have pizza, nachos, hot dogs, snacks, and hot cocoa. Special programs include movie nights, snowshoe treks, puppet shows, and opportunities to meet Oakie, the Oakland County mascot.

Field Tip

A lighted Kiddie Sledding Hill is located near the Fridge toboggan run. Bring your own sled.

The Fridge

The Fridge is a wild ride that makes kids long for winter's cold weather. Dress warmly and get ready to scream. While the staff provides the four-person toboggan, it's your responsibility to carry it up three flights of stairs to the top of the tower. This heightens your excitement and anticipation. Get settled (small children can nestle between adults), then rocket down a 55-foot drop and whoosh along 1,000 icy feet at speeds sometimes greater than 30 miles per hour. The whole ride takes only 30 seconds, much less time than your wait in line. But while you're screaming, time is suspended, and the ride seems longer. Teens love the Fridge at night, twinkling with colored lights; as they zip through the tunnel of lights, it seems otherworldly.

33

Go Box

20900 Oakwood Boulevard
Dearborn 48124

313-271-1620; groups, 313-982-6001.
www.thehenryford.org

Mid-Apr.–Oct. 31: 9:30–5 daily.
Nov. 1–Dec. 31: 9:30–5 Fri.–Sun.

$20 adults, $14 ages 5–12, $19 seniors,
free for children 4 & under. Fee for
each ride unless you purchase an unlim-
ited daily pass, $10 nonmembers, $9
members, free for children 4 & under.

Free in lot north of museum

2 years & up

My Notes

Fun Food

Travel back to a stagecoach inn in the mid-1800s at the Eagle Tavern for family-style dining. Waitresses in era dress serve you authentic era dishes, such as Italian macaroni and effervescing drinks. For a quicker meal, the cafeteria-style A Taste of History restaurant offers kids a hobo lunch—a sandwich, string cheese, and a cookie, held by a kerchief on a stick.

Find Southern goodies—such as fried okra, hush puppies, and catfish—at the outdoor Mrs. Fisher's Southern Cooking. Stop at the Guild Beer Hall to snack on buttery popcorn or roasted peanuts and drink cream soda or root beer from the tap. You'll find ice cream, cus-tard, and lemonade stands along Main Street and giant cookies and candy by the pound at Sir John Bennett Sweet Shop.

Field Tip

Be prepared. For little ones, you need a stroller or wagon to walk through the village. Bring hats, sunscreen, snacks, and water. Be sure to plan your visit by taking a few minutes when you arrive to read through the daily events and look at the village map. Save the Greenfield Village Store for the end. There you'll find a wide selection of historic gifts, games, coloring books, kits, clothes, cars, train paraphernalia, and dolls.

Greenfield Village

Greenfield Village brings history to life for kids and celebrates individual courage and ingenuity. Visit during Summer Festival, usually mid-June through August, and you'll find a village full of strolling costumed characters, reenactments in homes and farms, a play in the Town Hall, historic games on the Village Green, and historic baseball games at 1 p.m. each weekend. There are also special weekend festivals, including Motor Muster and Fourth of July concerts.

During Summer Festival, kids meet Orville and Wilbur Wright in their home and Thomas Edison in his Menlo Park Complex. They can ride a steam engine, Model T, or carousel. They learn about slavery at the Susquehanna Plantation and about life as freed former slaves at the Mattox Family Home. They can enjoy the Cotswold Cottage Tea, where children have their own drink and food. They can make a basket, candleholder, or glass flower in the Liberty Craftworks area. Or they can listen to stories and watch farm chores at the Firestone Farm.

Come back for Halloween in Greenfield Village, featuring 800 carved pumpkins, treat stations, elaborately dressed characters, storytelling, and the Haunted Horseman. In December, during Holiday Nights, the village is decked out in Victorian decor, with musical performances, storytelling, ice-skating, and fireworks. When the village opens in April, kids are invited to Meet Thomas the Tank Engine, a special event with storytelling, train rides, character meet and greet, and crafts.

Go Box

20900 Oakwood Boulevard
Dearborn 48124

313-271-1620; groups, 313-982-6001; IMAX movie hotline, 313-271-1570. www.thehenryford.org

9:30–5 daily year-round

$14 adults, $10 ages 5–12, $13 seniors, free for children 4 & under

Free in lot south of museum

3 & up

My Notes

Fun Food

Treat your mini-historians to the Michigan Café's Kid Cruiser meal, served in a cardboard vintage car. Kids have their choice of hot dog, chicken tenders, or PB&J, with chips and cookie or string cheese and applesauce. You'll also find macaroni & cheese and other hot or cold meals, drinks, and snacks, such as old-fashioned puddings, homemade apple strudel, and brownie sundaes, all served cafeteria style. Or enjoy a regular or jumbo foot-long hot dog with all the fixings in the Wienermobile Café. Fixings are serious and include—to name a few—chili, cheese, onions, and jalapeños for the Texas Dog; baked beans and cheese for the Beanie Wienie; and cheese sauce and tortilla chips for the Nacho Dogero.

Field Tip

Be sure to treat the kids to an IMAX movie experience. The Henry Ford IMAX Theatre offers both regular and 3-D IMAX movies (you need to put on black plastic glasses to have dinosaurs and rocks look like they are tumbling out of the screen to hit you on the head). You're in for a wow experience both visually and aurally, with a screen eight stories wide and six stories high and state-of-the-art, wraparound digital sound.

The Genius at Play store offers an assortment of books, kits, cars, and dolls—all innovative and educational—just for kids, starting off with baby toys. You'll also find a huge selection of gifts and souvenirs at the Henry Ford Museum Store.

Henry Ford Museum

This museum offers restless kids a spacious place to explore and learn about the American experience. Five of the permanent collections—Automobile in American Life, Your Place in Time, Made in America, Heroes of the Sky, and With Liberty and Justice for All—have special activities for kids.

All ages enjoy creating K'NEX cars in Automobile in American Life. Kids are encouraged to test their driving machines for speed and safety along a lane and down a ramp. While in this exhibit, pick up a "Pilot Log" scavenger hunt list from Lamy's Diner to use in Heroes of the Sky, where you will walk along an elevated viewing platform to see planes from on high.

Play with toys from other generations in Your Place in Time. There are Etch A Sketches, Mr. Potato Heads, and Lincoln Logs. Children can also pretend to be Madonna or the Pointer Sisters as they dance and sing in a karaoke setting and watch themselves on a screen.

The whole family can get into the act of creating model cars at the assembly line set up in Made in America. In Liberty and Justice for All, students in grades 4–12 can use their "Student Exploration Guide" to direct them through the exhibit and make rubbings. Be sure to go inside and listen to the audio at the Rosa Parks Bus and to stop at the Lincoln chair and Washington's camp bed.

Come back during December for a wonderful fairyland, gift-wrapped magically with toy trains and gingerbread houses and featuring hands-on crafts, stories, and Santa. Celebrate Black History Month in February with dramatic speeches, songs, hands-on crafts, and the actual bus where Rosa Parks made civil rights history. Macy's Second Mondays (10–noon the second Monday of each month) feature special activities and crafts for toddlers and free museum entrance for children younger than five.

Go Box

26750 23 Mile Road
Chesterfield 48051

586-949-4100, ext. 9108.
www.lionel.com/CentralStation/VisitorCenter

Tours: 10, 3, & 4 Wed. & Thurs.;
10, 1:30, & 2:30 Fri.; 10, 11, & noon Sat.
Reservations required. Gift shop:
1:30–4:30 Tues.–Fri., 10–12:30 Sat.

Free

Free on site

2 & up

My Notes

Fun Food

For those who love chain restaurants, M-59 (or Hall Road east of Van Dyke) is heaven. From the I-75 expressway on the west to the I-94 expressway on the east, there are almost 20 miles of uninterrupted chain restaurants (and chain stores). Take your pick of ribs, burgers, pasta, fried chicken, hot dogs, or tacos.

Field Tip

If your children have a sweet tooth, they will enjoy the Morley Candy Makers and Sanders Tour (23770 Hall Road, Clinton Township 48036), during which they can watch "Oompah Loompahs" in the candy kitchen through the large windows of an observation walkway. They will also enjoy the free sample at the end of the tour and, of course, buying candy at the gift shop. Call 586-468-4300 for free one-hour tour times. If you aren't part of a group, ask if you can join a small one.

Lionel Trains

All aboard! In 1900, Joshua Lionel Cowen opened a clothing store in New York City and put a motorized toy train car in his storefront window. Shoppers were interested more in the train than in his dry goods. The rest is history, and you can read this history on a 52-foot-long artifact wall at Lionel Trains. There are great photos of Joshua Lionel Cowen and his first trains.

But what captures kids the most are the bells and whistles of the interactive 14-by-40-foot train layout. There are 10–15 trains working simultaneously, chugging along villages and cities, through tunnels, and over bridges. Kids can press more than 30 buttons on this setup or run the trains themselves on the special kids-only, 6-by-8-foot train layout.

The hour-long free tour starts with a short video outlining the product and how Lionel began. The next stop is the railroad community, and the final destination is the gift shop, where you'll be hard-pressed to leave without at least one model train and a blue and white striped train engineer's cap.

Go Box

Oakland University, Rochester 48309. Entrance is west off Adams Road, just south of Walton Road

248-370-3140; group tours, 248-364-6224; Girl Scout programs, 248-364-6252. www2.oakland.edu/oakland/OUportal/index.asp?site=87

Guided tours daily after Mem. Day–Labor Day: 11:30, 12:30, 1:30, & 2:30. Guided tours Jan.–Mem. Day weekend & after Labor Day–Thanksgiving: 1:30 Mon.–Fri.; 11:30, 12:30, 1:30, & 2:30 Sat. & Sun. Holiday Walk: self-guided tours, 11–5 daily; guided tours with music and food, Thanksgiving weekend–Christmas. Girl Scout programs year-round, 4:30 Mon.–Thurs.; 10, 1, & 4 Sat.

Guided tours: $15 adults, $10 seniors, free for children 12 & under

Free on site

5 & up

Fun Food

Sit at the counter and swing your legs while you enjoy burgers, fries, grilled cheese sandwiches, and old-fashioned chocolate malts at Knapp's Dairy Barn (304 Main St., 248-651-4545).

Field Tip

Stop at Halfway Down the Stairs Children's Book Shop (114 E. Fourth St., 248-652-6066), a wonderful, independently owned children's bookstore.

If your kids are into nature or history, you'll want to explore two sites in adjacent Rochester Hills: Dinosaur Hill Nature Preserve (333 N. Hill Circle, 48307; 248-656-0999) and Rochester Hills Museum at the Van Hoosen Farm (1005 Van Hoosen Rd., 48309; 248-656-4663). Both offer classes, summer camps, and special events.

My Notes

Meadow Brook Hall

Meadow Brook Hall is the Michigan equivalent to North Carolina's Biltmore Estate. The country's fourth largest historic house museum, it was built between 1926 and 1929 by Matilda Dodge Wilson (widow of auto pioneer John Dodge) and her second husband, lumber baron Alfred G. Wilson. It's a 110-room, 88,000-square-foot mansion, complete with original furnishings and art. The house tour isn't for small children (in fact, strollers have to be checked at the cloakroom), but older children with a fondness for romantic history will enjoy the rich furnishings and stories. The mansion offers six Girl Scout programs for all levels, beginning with five year olds; each program includes a badge or patch, dress-up time, and a tea consisting of lemonade and cookies.

During the Holiday Walk, Santa presides over Knole Cottage, a six-room playhouse built to three-quarter size for the Wilson daughter. Kids will want to explore this cottage.

If your children ask to see more homes of auto barons, visit the Henry Ford Estate—Fair Lane (4901 Evergreen Rd., Dearborn 48128; 313-593-5590), the Edsel and Eleanor Ford House (100 Lake Shore Rd., Grosse Pointe Shores 48236; 313-884-4222), or the Fisher Mansion (383 Lenox, Detroit 48215; 313-331-6740). All three home tours bring the owners and their families to life with stories and offer special events and programs.

Go Box

30300 Hales
Madison Heights 48071

248-585-0100.
www.ci.madison-heights.mi.us (click on
"Community," then "Attractions," then
"DPS—Nature Center Division")

10–6 Tues. & Thurs., noon–8 Wed.,
10–5 Fri., noon–5 Sat. & Sun.
Trails open dawn to dusk.

Free

Free on site

All ages

My Notes

Fun Food

Order breakfast any time of day at The Breakfast Club (30600 John R, Madison Heights; 248-307-9090), a cozy place to take kids for comfort food, such as pancakes, waffles, omelets, and grilled cheese.

Field Tip

The Nature Center offers birthday parties and a variety of classes, workshops, and day camps. You'll also find wildflower walks, bird-watching, Saturday-morning movies, and summertime hot dog lunches on Fridays. Call to be placed on the mailing list.

See pond life—frogs, turtles, fish, and aquatic insects—up close. The Environmental Discovery Center at Indian Springs Metropark (5200 Indian Trail, White Lake 48386; 800-477-3192 or 248-625-7280) allows you to walk underneath a pond through a Plexiglas dome.

Nature Center at Friendship Woods

Nestled in the midst of nearly 40 acres of the George W. Suarez Friendship Woods, this small nature center in a log cabin is a perfect place to take small children for their first introduction to nature. Friendly volunteers enjoy sharing their knowledge with kids and letting them explore. Kids can touch and feel fur, hides, skin, bones, and skeletons and view aquariums full of snakes, turtles, and fish. There are live animals and taxidermy mounts. There is a computer inside a small cave, and there are lots of seasonal nature displays. A small gift shop sells snacks and nature gifts that make great stocking stuffers or party favors. On a sunny day, you can take a stroll on marked trails through the woods.

Go Box

581 State Circle
Ann Arbor 48108

734-994-4420. www.scrapbox.org

10–6 Tues.–Fri., 10–2 Sat.

$5 for a large bag of artistic scraps, $3 for a small bag. There are also inexpensive arts & crafts supplies and kits for sale.

Free on site

2 & up

My Notes

Fun Food

After shopping or creating at a workshop, bring your hungry children next door to Mark's Midtown Coney Island (3672 State St., 734-747-6707), where they can eat breakfast any time of day or choose salads, sandwiches, and soups at modest prices.

Field Tip

A similar nonprofit store in Detroit is Arts and Scraps (16135 Harper Ave., 48224; 313-640-4411), offering artistic scraps, kits, workshops, classes, birthday parties, and scout badges.

Show your little ones work by real artists at the University of Michigan Museum of Art (1301 S. University Ave., Ann Arbor 48104; 734-763-8662; www.umma.umich.edu), which is occupying a small temporary exhibition space during restoration and renovation, scheduled to be complete in fall 2009.

The Scrap Box

The Scrap Box has made recycling artistic. You can shop at this nonprofit store for scraps that have been recycled from businesses and manufacturers—remnants, samples, cutouts, and seconds. Picture bins and bins of tubes, punchboard, foam tubes, Styrofoam shapes, paper of all sizes and colors, and carpet, fabric, and wallpaper swatches. Crafty moms, preschool teachers, Sunday school teachers, and scout leaders will recognize good scraps and turn this useful material into learning games, projects, mobiles, and puppets. Sample projects and ideas are on display around the store, just in case your creative genes need a push.

The Scrap Box offers birthday parties, field trips, drop-in activities during school vacation, and classes and workshops for adults and children. Up to 60 people can be accommodated.

Go Box

441 Monroe Avenue
Detroit 48226

Tours, 313-961-0325;
general information,
313-961-0920.
www.secondbaptistdetroit.org

Tours by appointment only

$5 adults, $3 ages 12 & under

Park on street or use structures
in Greektown

8 & up

My Notes

Fun Food

Walk one block east on Monroe to the heart of Greektown and have your pick of Greek restaurants, including New Parthenon (547 Monroe, 313-961-5111), New Hellas Cafe (583 Monroe, 313-961-5544), and Pegasus Taverna (558 Monroe, 313-964-6800). Be sure to stop for baklava and other Greek baked goods at Astoria Pastry (541 Monroe, 313-963-9603).

Field Tip

Learn the role Ann Arbor played on the Underground Railroad with tours given by the African American Cultural and Historical Museum of Washtenaw County (1100 North Main St., Ann Arbor 48104; 734-996-0603).

The Second Baptist Church in Detroit, established in 1836 by 13 former slaves, soon became a stop on the Underground Railroad. From 1836 to 1865, more than 5,000 fugitive slaves passed through the 12-by-13-foot windowless, cellar room. They stayed in the claustrophobic room with a dirt floor for a day or two, until it was safe to be bundled in the bottom of a hay wagon and driven at night to the banks of the Detroit River. A ferry took them across to Canada and to freedom. Detroit was known to the fugitives as "Midnight," because it was the end of the line, ultimately leading to Canada.

Many famous African Americans have addressed the congregation regarding slavery and abolition, including Sojourner Truth, John Brown, and Frederick Douglass. On the tour, learn about the history of the church and its famous members, then continue down a narrow staircase into the once barren room. Colorful murals now tell the story of the church's role on the Underground Railroad.

Go Box

Jewish Community Center
6600 West Maple Road
West Bloomfield 48322

877-742-5663.
www.shalomstreet.org

Noon–5 Mon.–Thurs., 1–5 Sun. Extended hours during school vacations. Group visits are scheduled Sun.–Thurs.; call for an appointment.

Suggested donation: $5/person, $18 family

Free on site

3–12

My Notes

Fun Food

Milk and Honey (248-661-2327), located in the Jewish Community Center, right across from Shalom Street, is an upscale kosher dairy restaurant.

Field Tip

If it's a warm day, make time to play on Shalom Playground, located north of the building, near the Drake Road entrance. Here you'll find everything for infants and toddlers: baby swings, a teeter-totter with four seats, a bouncy airplane, sandy areas and toys, and two climbers—one with a bridge, for older children; one with a truck steering wheel, for younger children. Ringing the whole playground are benches for watchful parents or grandparents.

To learn all about health, go to the Saint Joseph Mercy Health Exploration Station (1600 South Canton Center Rd., Suite 10, Canton 48188; 734-398-7518; www.healthexplorationstation.com), a creative playscape made up of parts of the body.

Shalom Street

Shalom Street is designed as an interactive museum of Jewish life, culture, and values. It offers both high-tech and low-tech displays to explore the core Jewish value of Tikun Olam (tee-koon oh-lam), loosely interpreted as "fixing the world." Tikun Olam encourages kids to make their home, community, natural environment, and relationships with loved ones and strangers as whole, calm, and positive as possible.

In the Adventure Travel exhibit space, kids can mug in front of the video camera and turn up on a television screen as visitors to many different countries. They can plunk their coins into a *tzedakah* box (used to collect coins for charity), here designed as a noisy, colorful Rube Goldberg contraption of levers and pulleys on a wall.

At the Home exhibit, they can build a home's foundation by choosing from bricks inscribed with such words as "respect," "not bullying," or "seek peace." A phone in the exhibit tells a story with an ethical dilemma, and they can decide what they would do about cheating or squealing on friends. Inside the home, they can use their sense of smell to try to identify foods. In a quiet corner, they can relax with books and puzzles and play with seasonal holiday toys.

In addition, there are craft tables and space for traveling exhibits, live entertainment, and birthday parties. School and community groups are encouraged to visit for teaching diversity.

Go Box

Max M. Fisher Music Center
3711 Woodward Avenue
Detroit 48201

313-576-5111; groups, 313-576-5130.
www.detroitsymphony.com

Saturdays, Nov.–Apr.: Tiny Tots Concert
Series in the Music Box, 10:30; Young
People's Concert Series in Orchestra Hall,
10 & 11:30; KidZone activities in the
atrium, 9–11:30.

Tiny Tots concerts, $12 each; Young
People's concerts, $10–$27 each

$7 in parking garage on the Music Center's
south side

Tiny Tots concerts, 3–6; Young People's
concerts, 6 & up

My Notes

Fun Food

For fantastic upscale brunch food, try Detroit's Breakfast House
and Grill (1241 Woodward, 313-961-1115).

Field Tip

Come to Meadow Brook Music Festival during July–August,
when the Detroit Symphony Orchestra plays. Your kids will love
staying up late, lying on blankets, and watching the stars while
they listen to music.

Super Saturdays at the Max

Super Saturdays at the Max combine Tiny Tots concerts and Young People's concerts on the same day, with KidZone activities held in between the concerts. On any Super Saturday, the Max is full of youngsters and their parents and grandparents. There is a palpable excitement and high noise level in the Music Center's atrium lobby and halls.

KidZone spreads its hands-on activities onto each of the three levels of the center. There are face painters, clowns making elaborate balloon animals and hats, and tables of crayons and coloring sheets. Kids can try playing instruments and meet Thomas Wilkins, maestro of the Young People's Concert Series. There are also kid-oriented foods, such as Rice Krispy treats, hot dogs, mini-muffins, juice boxes, and milk.

Tiny Tots concerts in the intimate Music Box are informal. While they are geared toward children ages 3–6, many families bring along their infants to 2 year olds. You can sit on pads on the floor near the stage or in chairs in the back of the small room. The show goes on while families go back and forth from the floor to the chairs, kids cry, parents feed infants their bottles, and little ones eat Cheerios and other snacks. The entertainers—usually a combination of local and national children's performers—know their audience's quirks and sing and perform in loud voices and elicit audience participation.

The Young People's Concert Series is a bit more formal. It's held in the proper Orchestra Hall, where children are expected to mind their concert manners. Yet Maestro Wilkins has fun with his youthful audience, talks right to them, gets them to participate, and doesn't expect them to sit perfectly still. This concert series, featuring the Detroit Symphony Orchestra, usually offers a learning experience for parents and children.

Go Box

1702 Scott Lake Road
Waterford 48328

248-858-4625; recorded message,
248-858-0918. www.splashfun.com

Mem. Day–Labor Day: 11–7 daily.
July: 11–8 daily.

Oakland County nonresidents: $16 for over
43 inches tall, $10 for 30–43 inches tall.
Oakland County residents: $12 for over 43
inches tall, $8 for 30–43 inches tall. Free for
children under 30 inches. Twilight discounts
after 4. Group rates available.

Free on site

All ages

My Notes

Fun Food

Bring your own picnic or buy kid-pleasing concession food—ice cream, pizza, fries, nachos, hot dogs, and pop. There are shady picnic tables spread around the area, some even in a covered area.

Field Tip

Southeast Michigan has an indoor water park at the Warren Community Center in Warren (5460 Arden, 586-268-8400) and a variety of outdoor water parks:

Belle Isle Waterslides, Belle Isle Park, Detroit 48207; 313-852-4059.
Chandler Park Family Aquatic Center, 12600 Chandler Park Dr., Detroit 48213; 313-822-7665.
Groveland Oaks Waterslide, 5990 Grange Hall Rd., Holly 48442; 248-634-9811.
Indian Springs Metropark, 5200 Indian Trail, White Lake 48386; 248-625-7280.
Kensington Metropark, 2240 W. Buno Rd., Milford 48380; 800-477-3178.
Lake Erie Metropark Wave Pool, 32481 W. Jefferson, Brownstown 48173; 734-379-5020.
Metro Beach Metropark, 31300 Metropolitan Parkway, Mt. Clemens 48046; 586-463-4581.
Red Oaks Waterpark, 1455 E. 13 Mile Rd., Madison Heights 48071; 248-585-6990.
Rolling Hills Family Water Park, 7660 Stony Creek Rd., Ypsilanti 48197; 734-484-9655.
Southgate Splash Park, 16777 Northline Rd., Southgate 48195; 734-282-9622.
Troy Family Aquatic Center, 3425 Civic Center Dr., Troy 48084; 248-524-3514.
Veterans Park Waterslide, 2150 Jackson Rd., Ann Arbor 48107; 734-761-7240.

Waterford Oaks Wave Pool and Waterslide

There are some hot summer days when you can only sufficiently cool off at the nearest water park. Pack up the kids, a cooler full of snacks and water, sunscreen, towels, hats, and sunglasses. Come early to get a spot and an inner tube for the wave-action pool.

Waterford Oaks is a water park with all the amenities. The Big Bucket children's water playground features more than 30 interactive activities, including a colorful plastic climbing playground with waterfalls, sprays, and a giant bucket that tips water on screaming kids every few minutes. Parents can set their chairs in the shallow water at the periphery of the area and keep an eye on their children.

If you are at least 43 inches tall, you can go on the Slidewinder waterslides and whoosh down 340 feet into the warm water of the wave-action pool; once in the pool, you can body surf the three-foot waves or hop onto a park-owned tube to ride wild waves as they alternate with calm ones. Or, if you are at least 30 inches tall, you can choose to go on Ragin' Rapids, a four-person raft ride that starts at a height of three stories and drops 515 feet through twists and turns, ending in a three-foot-deep splashdown pool.

Waterford Oaks also offers a bathhouse, swim lessons, and birthday parties.

Mid-Michigan

Go Box

Midland Center for the Arts
1801 West St. Andrews
Midland 48640

989-631-5930 or 800-523-7649.
www.mcfta.org

10–5 Tues.–Sat., 1–5 Sun.

$5 adults, $3 ages 14 & under,
free for children 3 & under

Free on site

5 & up

My Notes

Fun Food

You'll find gifts and chocolates on Main Street. For an informal lunch of pizza or sandwiches or for an ice cream snack, go to Pizza Sam's (102 W. Main St., 989-631-1934).

Field Tip

Midland Center for the Arts also offers a children's theater series and the Midland Symphony Orchestra's Tunes for Tots concerts. For schedules, call 800-523-7649.

Drive downtown and let the kids run across The Tridge, one of Midland's famous landmarks. This reddish-brown three-pronged bridge is located on Ashman, behind the Farmer's Market.

Nestled in the Midland Center for the Arts is the modern Alden B. Dow Museum of Science and Art, chock-full of hands-on exhibits for curious children. Set up like a kaleidoscope of learning, there's a little of everything you'd find in the art, historical, or natural science museums in big cities.

What kids see first is the giant mastodon skeleton with huge tusks. Then, as they wind up the stairs to the next level, they learn about Michigan's environment, with push-and-smell fragrances of sassafras, maple, cherry, pine, and wintergreen. There are videos and walk-into environments about Michigan's Native peoples, logging, farming, and copper mining. For instance, you are asked to press down on a TNT box to detonate an explosion in a copper mine. Chemistry buffs will enjoy a section on how chemistry is a huge part of Dow Chemical's ability to create new products.

The third level is the Hall of Ideas, one exhibit after another that blends art and science and asks kids to try puzzles, look at photographs, create a mobile and computer art, try their hand at calligraphy and movable type, and listen to music or instruments in a music studio and a sound room. There's even a small theater to learn about the origins of the motion picture. The fourth level is a gallery space of changing exhibits.

The museum's gift shop is a great place to spend birthday money. There are science and art kits, including kits for pirate and dinosaur lovers, plus picture books, coloring books, stickers, tattoos, and plush toys. Kids can sign up for science and art classes and summer camps. The museum also offers school programs and scout badge workshops, and there is an outdoor Summer Art Fair the first weekend in June.

Go Box

1221 East Kearsley Street
Flint 48503

810-237-3450.
www.sloanmuseum.com

10–5 Mon.–Fri., noon–5 Sat. & Sun.

$6 adults, $5 ages 3–11, free for
children 2 & under

Free on site

5 & up

My Notes

Fun Food

It's fun to sit in the museum's Halfway Café, a 1950s diner, and have a snack and drink. But for a good selection of soups, salads, sandwiches, and snacks, walk across the Cultural Center Mall to the Flint Institute of Arts Café (810-234-1695). Art Institute admission is free unless there is a special exhibit. You don't have to pay admission to go to the café.

Field Tip

The Sloan Museum is located on the grounds of the Flint Cultural Center (www.flintculturalcenter.org), along with the Flint Institute of Arts, Longway Planetarium, Flint Youth Theatre, and The Whiting. If you are going to visit, it pays to check what's on tap at each site. For kids, highlights of the recently renovated and expanded Flint Institute of Arts feature a contemporary sculpture courtyard and the modern galleries. Be sure to see the Duane Hanson sculptures, plus once-a-year special traveling shows. Longway Planetarium offers laser and star shows, and both the Flint Youth Theatre and The Whiting have a schedule of family and children's plays.

Alfred P. Sloan Museum

The Sloan Museum offers a fun romp through the first half of 20th-century Flint, with posters and artifacts from Ya-Ya's, Halo Burger, and the General Motors car plant. In the Discovery Center, kids can play with blocks and toys and experiment with science. Usually, a traveling exhibit takes up several galleries and offers hands-on play and demonstrations. For kids, the best part of the museum may be the gift shop, loaded with old-fashioned whistles, magnets, stickers, kitchen chemistry kits, books, puzzles, puppets, and lots of toy cars.

Go Box

1730 South Washington Avenue
Saginaw 48601

989-759-1408. www.saginawzoo.com

May–Sept.: 10–5 Mon.–Sat., 10–8 Wed.,
11–6 Sun. & holidays. Oct.: weekends
only; Dec.: holiday hours.

$7 adults & children, free for infants–11
months. Carousel and train: $2/person for
one ride, free for infants–11 months.

Free on site

Infants–10 years

My Notes

Fun Food

Bring your lunch and eat at one of the picnic tables, or buy your lunch or a snack at one of the zoo's two concessions, which sell hot dogs, popcorn, cotton candy, and ice cream. Drive about four and a half miles southwest to Fuzzy's (1924 Court St., 989-790-1719) for burgers or pizza.

Field Tip

Teach your children to appreciate simplicity, respect nature, and trust diversity at the Japanese Cultural Center (527 Ezra Rust Dr., 989-759-1648). Groups can schedule a children's tour that includes drinking green tea and eating sweets, practicing origami, and learning about a kimono by trying one on. Families are welcome year-round every second Saturday at 2 p.m. for a formal tea ceremony. Families can also take a self-guided walk through the gardens from April through September.

Children's Zoo at Celebration Square

This small zoo is set up for young children and well worth the visit. Kids will see about two dozen animal species up close. The zoo grounds are colorful and full of flowers. Families can hop on a red, open-air train chugging around the perimeter of the park. They can also ride an old-fashioned carousel of hand-carved and hand-painted animals. They can watch daily animal shows in the outdoor Amphitheater, and they can pet and feed animals in the Barnyard. What more do kids want from a zoo? Maybe ice cream and cotton candy. It's all at the Children's Zoo.

There are alligators, bald eagles, bobcats, and butterflies; macaws, monkeys, and wolves; prairie dogs, emus, and otters. Check at the entrance for the daily list of feeding times, shows, and demonstrations. The train ride is breezy on a summer's day, and the carousel lifts your spirits. The zoo offers special events, such as Halloween Harvest Zoo Boo and Holidays at the Zoo, plus ice cream socials, concerts, birthday parties, scout workshops, camp, and group visits.

Go Box

6140 Bray Road
Flint 48505

800-648-7275 or 810-736-7100.
www.geneseecountyparks.org/
crossroadsvillage.htm

Mem. Day–Labor Day:
10–5 Wed.–Sun.

Village only: $9 ages 13–59, $7 ages
25 months–12 years, $8 seniors,
free for children 24 months & under.
Additional fees for Huckleberry
Railroad & *Genesee Belle* rides.

Free on site

All ages

My Notes

Fun Food

The village offers three casual restaurant choices. At the Crossroads Café, you'll find sandwiches, ice cream, and other snacks. The Mill Street Warehouse offers cafeteria-style salads, sandwiches, soups, and snacks. The Lakeside Grill, with a view of Mott Lake, serves burgers, grilled sandwiches, hot dogs, and corn dogs. The *Genesee Belle* also offers snacks and beverages.

Field Tip

In October, dress the kids in their costumes and enjoy a spooky train ride through a haunted forest and a Halloween magic show in the opera house during Halloween Ghost and Goodies (noon–9 weekends, 5–9 weekdays).

Nothing beats walking through a snow-covered historic village while gentle snowflakes fall (sometimes Mother Nature doesn't cooperate). Your kids will want to make an annual event of Christmas at Crossroads (4–9 Wed.–Sun., Nov. 24–Dec. 30). Take a train ride through the glittery forest decorated with 600,000 sparkling lights, walk through the decorated village, watch the holiday show at the opera house, visit with Santa, and enjoy a model train exhibit and craft demonstrations.

Crossroads Village and Huckleberry Railroad

Crossroads Village and Huckleberry Railroad is one of the best-kept secrets in Michigan. It's perfect for families with small children. It was the first successful all-day outing we took when our twins were two years old and their older brother was five. Be sure to hop aboard the full-size steam engine on the Huckleberry Railroad for a 40-minute breezy ride through the scenic Genesee Recreation Area. Take the kids on the *Genesee Belle* paddle wheeler for a 45-minute boat ride on Lake Mott. From Memorial Day to Labor Day, the village offers themed weekends, hosting costumed musicians and craftspeople who interact with visitors and demonstrate old-fashioned pleasures, chores, and crafts.

Bring your wagon or stroller and explore the village. Stop at a few of the 34 buildings, ride the colorful 1912 Parker hand-carved carousel and the restored 1910 Parker Superior Wheel (a Ferris wheel), swing on the boat-shaped Venetian swings, ride a miniature train and mechanical pony carts, have an ice cream, and just take in the warmth of a low-tech summer day.

Kids will enjoy the working cider mill, the one-room schoolhouse, and many of the houses offering craft demonstrations. When you arrive, be sure to find out about the shows in the Colwell Opera House and if there are timed children's activities.

Go Box

1809 Eastman Avenue
Midland 48640

989-631-2677 or 800-362-4874.
www.dowgardens.org

9 to one hour before sunset daily
year-round

$5 adults, $1 ages 6–17, free for
children 5 & under

Free on site

All ages

My Notes

Fun Food

For breakfast food any time of day and in hearty portions, eat at Omeletes & More (112 E. Main St., 989-839-0930).

Field Tip

Whiting Forest (989-837-8299 or 800-362-4874), located north of Dow Gardens on Eastman Ave., offers trails and native Michigan forest environments, plus story times and seasonal experiences, such as honey tasting.

Dow Gardens—Children's Garden

Dow Gardens is a peaceful oasis of streams, red bridges, huge rocks, trees, and flowers. Kids will love romping around and running over the brightly colored bridges. Most of all, they will enjoy fooling around in the Children's Garden. A short, five-minute stroll from the visitor center, colorful circles announce the garden. At its center is a wooden fort with a green tiled roof and stairs on two sides. There are also pergolas, a little barnyard of animals, and a wild boar sculpture. Depending on the season, there will be flowers and garden plots or a corn maze and scarecrow. If you visit during mid-March to mid-April, enjoy colorful butterflies indoors in the conservatory.

Dow Gardens is extremely friendly to children, offering strolls, classes, story times, camp, family experiences, and seasonal events. The gift shop has a children's area selling paraphernalia for backyard exploration, gardening, and outdoor play, plus books, stickers, puzzles, and clothes.

Go Box

1602 West Third Avenue
Flint 48504

810-767-5437.
www.flintchildrensmuseum.org

9–5 Tues.–Sat.

$4 adults & children, free for
children under 1

Free on site

Infants–9 years

My Notes

Fun Food

Although I'm not a huge advocate of feeding children fast food, I have to mention Flint's famous Halo Burger chain (810-767-0022, www.haloburger.com). It was started in 1923, and everyone who grew up in or near Flint knows that you haven't lived until you've experienced a green-olive burger and a Boston cooler. Or you can just order a plain burger and milk shake. There are 10 drive-through restaurants (plus one that's sit-down only) in the Flint area.

Field Tip

The museum offers birthday parties, field trips, group workshops, scout badge programs, and special events in cooperation with other institutions, such as when a new traveling exhibit comes to the Flint Institute of Arts.

Flint's Children's Museum

On the outside, Flint's Children's Museum looks like a castle, with gold-capped turrets. This theme continues as children step inside and use their imagination, becoming storybook princesses and princes. In the Center Stage area, they'll find a Cinderella stagecoach, giant storybook, castle stage, puppet theater, throne, and dragon. There are lots of puppets to play with and costumes to try on. After creating their own play, kids can watch it on a television monitor. The music room is inviting, with unconventional instruments created from found objects, such as trash cans and plastic caps.

The museum offers a Health and Fitness area, with a climbing wall, treadmill, and exercycle; a Mr. Bones skeleton that shows kids how their bones move; and Stuffee, a five-foot-tall stuffed character with removable heart, lungs, stomach, and other organs.

Kids can also pretend to go shopping at a grocery store and practice their fractions at a pizza restaurant. They can put on firefighter clothes and learn street signs and how to obey traffic signals.

A Tot Spot just for children under three is located away from the fray. It has a colorful crawl-through area, large LEGOs, and a quiet space with a rocking chair, perfect for moms who have infants and want to watch their older toddlers play.

Go Box

200 Museum Drive
Lansing 48933

517-485-8116.
www.impression5.org

10–5 Mon.–Sat., 10–8 Thurs.,
1–5 Sun.

$5 adults, $4 ages 3 & up & seniors,
free for children 2 & under

Free on site

2 & up

My Notes

Fun Food

Drive just a few miles east to Okemos for great stuffed pizza, calzones, and specialty pizzas at Old Chicago (1938 W. Grand Blvd., 48864; 517-347-1111). Or eat downtown on Washington (see Michigan Historical Museum).

Field Tip

Riverwalk Theatre, located next to Impression 5 Science Center, offers several children's shows each season. For a brochure, call 517-482-5700.

The Nokomis Museum (5153 Marsh Road, Okemos), a small Native American Cultural Center, is dedicated to giving groups a hands-on understanding of the history, arts, and culture of the People of the Three Fires—the Ottawa, Potawatomi, and Ojibway. For a group workshop, call 517-349-5777.

Impression 5 Science Center

Picture a huge warehouse filled with color, light, pulleys, musical instruments, a heart maze, and a whisper dish. That's Impression 5 Science Center. In this spacious one-floor center, kids are encouraged to play, discover, and explore. You can keep an eye on your kids as they skip from display to display. They can wear an apron and navigate a ship in the Water Room; make music on a giant xylophone, cello, and player piano; find their way out of the heart maze; test their shots in a simulated basketball cage; or create a gigantic bubble in the Bubble Room. Toddlers have their own room, with a puppet stage, a house, and lots of toys. Kids can also make slime daily in the Chemistry Lab.

This center has a huge gift shop, offering some things other science centers don't have, such as kits for a crime lab, a radio, and a jet racer, as well as kits on air pressure. The shop also has rocks, marbles, astronaut ice cream, rubber and plush animals, dinosaurs, and books. Serious science students will find periodic tables. The center also offers homeschool programs, school and scout badge workshops, camps, overnight adventures, birthday parties, and special Saturday and Sunday programs.

Go Box

301 South Superior Street
Albion 49224

517-624-8023. www.kidsnstuff.org

School year: 10–5 Tues., Wed., Fri.;
11–6 Thurs. & Sat. Open more hours
in the summer and during holidays.

$4 adults and children ages 1 & up

Free on street

Infants–9 years

My Notes

Fun Food

If you want an unusual dining experience that is all turkey all the time, drive 15 miles to Cornwell's Turkeyville USA (18935 15½ Mile Road, Marshall 49068; 800-228-4315; www.turkeyville.com). Turkeyville features a turkey restaurant with great turkey sandwiches and hot turkey with all the fixings, an ice cream parlor with turkey-themed sundaes, and a gift shop/general store with breads, candies, fudge, and all sorts of down-home gifts. There's also a playground, 50 turkeys (although gobblers disappear as Thanksgiving gets closer), and rabbits and goats for children to pet. This is the perfect outing if you want your toddler to know what a turkey says.

Field Tip

I found three other children's museums in my travels, each more creative than the other, each offering so many imaginative displays that they made my head spin. See Flint's Children's Museum, Grand Rapids Children's Museum, and St. Joseph's Curious Kids Museum. Kids in these towns are lucky. You need to make the museums a focal point of your travels.

Kids 'N' Stuff Museum

This museum is a perfect spot for small children's creative exploration, craft making, imaginative play, and subliminal diversity training. There are so many thematic sections in this storefront play area that your child will have to come many times to experience all of them.

There is a little bit of everything and lots of space. You'll find a cultural dig in a sand table, with fossils and toys of the past; a music room with a drum set, organ tubes, pipes, and hand instruments; a messy-crafts room with supplies, a stamping area, and a chalk table; a toddler area with plastic kitchen food, trains, books, large blocks, animals, and LEGOs; a computer area with instructional games; a theater with costumes and a television green screen; a grocery store with real (but empty) boxes, cash registers, and carts; a climbing wall; a water world with aprons and boats; a world village featuring four countries, with costumes, food, language, books, and visuals; and even a sensory room, all in white, where children with autism can go to be quiet and relax.

Kids 'N' Stuff offers group visits, birthday parties, camps, classes, workshops, scout badges, and overnights.

Go Box

717 West Allegan
Lansing 48918

517-373-3559.
www.michiganhistory.org

9–4:30 Mon.–Fri., 10–4 Sat., 1–5 Sun.

Free

75 cents for 2 hours weekdays (pay at kiosk near museum), free on weekends

8 & up

My Notes

Fun Food

The place to be for lunch is on Washington, where the street is cobbled and you'll find a secondhand bookshop and dollar store besides lots of restaurants. My favorite is the Spotted Dog Café (221 S. Washington, 48933; 517-485-7574), a cafeteria-style restaurant with coffee drinks. Friendly employees make sandwiches and salads to order—you name it and they've got it. There are also dog biscuits available if your dog is hungry. Be sure to stop in The Peanut Shop (117 S. Washington, 517-374-0008). Since 1937, they've roasted peanuts in two old-fashioned roasters still working in the shop. Take home candies and nuts of all kinds by the pound.

Field Tip

Take a tour of the Capitol Building (9–4 Mon.–Fri.). For groups, call 517-373-2353.

Be sure to cheer on the Lansing Lugnuts in their colorful stadium in Oldsmobile Park. It's minor league baseball up close and personal. For tickets and schedules, call 517-485-4500.

Michigan Historical Center

This is a must-do for children either before they go into fourth grade or just after. If you have a fourth grader, you know that this is the year they do their Michigan project and report, so a trip to the capital city with the family (we aren't counting the squirming, noisy bus ride to the capital with their class) is required. The Michigan Historical Museum has done a wonderful job telling the story of Michigan and integrating past and present, diverse people, and Detroit and outstate stories. In fact, if you've traveled around the state, you will marvel at how well this museum represents what you'll find in West Michigan, Detroit, or Upper Peninsula historic museums.

More than two dozen galleries on four levels tell the story of Michigan from prehistory to 1975. Highlights are the walk-through environments, including a dark coal mine, elegant lumber baron's mansion, and 1920s theater where you can sit down and watch footage of Detroit in the 1920s. The museum also creates a cozy 1930s Ferndale bungalow, a former car plant that has become a World War II tank plant and is decorated with Rosie the Riveter posters, a sleek 1957 auto show with cars of the era, and a Motown recording studio where kids sing karaoke-style to Stevie Wonder or Martha Reeves and the Vandellas.

An incredible selection in the gift shop includes everything from maps, calendars, magnets, and flags to canoe-making kits, coloring books, cars, dolls, harmonicas, and Civil War mementoes.

Go Box

Michigan State University
West Circle Drive
East Lansing 48824

517-355-2370; recorded information,
517-355-7474. http://museum.msu.edu

9–5 Mon.–Fri., 10–5 Sat., 1–5 Sun.

$4 adults; free for children, students,
& faculty

$1 for 2 hours; parking permit must be
purchased at the gift shop & displayed
inside your car

8 & up

My Notes

Fun Food

For the creamiest ice cream (choose from 32 flavors), for chocolate cheese (a specialty since 1968), and for great grilled cheese sandwiches (what else did you expect?), come to the MSU Dairy Store. All ice cream and cheese are made right on campus. There are green tables and ice cream parlor chairs at the larger of the two stores, in Anthony Hall on Farm Lane (517-355-8466). A satellite store is in the MSU Union (571-353-9988). You can also find chain restaurants selling pizza, wraps, Mexican, Chinese, sandwiches, and sushi along Grand River on campus.

Field Tip

Meet cows, pigs, horses, sheep, and poultry at the Michigan State University Barns, open for group tours (call 517-355-8383). For tours of the Bug House, call 517-355-4662. The Children's 4-H Garden, with a tree house and themed gardens, such as a Giant's Garden and a Pizza Garden, is handicapped accessible and open for self-guided tours (call 517-355-5191).

Go Spartans! Cheer on your MSU teams. For tickets to sporting events, call the Michigan State University Athletic Office, 517-355-1610.

Curious elementary students will be rewarded by this small three-level teaching museum, chock-full of displays patiently explained by labels simple enough for children to understand. Highlights include the giant brown bear on the main level and a collections exhibit where children can open drawers to find Alaskan ivory, fossils, or chocolate molds and can engage in such questions as "How do we decide what collections to keep?" (the underlying theme of the museum).

Kids peek into a fur trader's cabin, printer's shop, and general store in the main level's Heritage Hall. In the Hall of World Cultures, on the ground level, kids find a hodgepodge of diverse objects, including Chinese dolls, Hmong quilts, Javanese shadow puppets, Odawa straw baskets, and a diorama of the Aztecs' capital city.

On the second level, there are dinosaur skeletons and elephant and mammoth skulls, plus lots of animal taxidermies. There's a small area to get cozy, play games, and read.

The gift shop has a huge selection of children's toys—musical instruments, Petoskey stones, Egyptian paraphernalia, books, kits, puppets, skeletons, kaleidoscopes, and miniature dinosaurs and animals.

For MSU fans, it is never too early to indoctrinate your children with a visit to campus. Be sure to stop at the Union for MSU paraphernalia.

Go Box

1301 South Pennsylvania Avenue
Lansing 48912

517-702-4221; recorded message,
517-483-4222. www.potterparkzoo.org

Spring & fall: 9–5 daily. Summer, 9–7 daily.
Winter, 10–5 daily.

Mar.–Oct.: Lansing residents, $4 adults, $2
children & seniors; nonresidents, $6 adults,
$2 children, $3 seniors. Nov.–Feb.: free
admission & parking.

$3

All ages

My Notes

Fun Food

Two zoo concessions—one near the entrance and one located near the bighorn sheep and African lion—serve all the outdoor food kids adore, including ice cream, hamburgers, hot dogs, and chicken fingers. If you prefer, stow a picnic lunch in your stroller, then sit at the picnic tables and augment lunch with drinks and dessert.

Field Tip

If your children love creepy crawly animals, visit the Minibeast Zooseum and Education Center (6907 West Grand River Ave., Watertown Twp. 48906; 517-886-0630; http://members.aol.com/YESbugs/zooseum.html), a small house run by the Young Entomologists Society. You'll find bugs, butterflies, moths, roaches, spiders, and insects of all sizes, colors, and shapes. Call ahead for spring–fall hours. The gift shop sells bug-collecting paraphernalia, books, specimens, and lollipops with edible bugs inside.

Potter Park Zoo

Potter Park Zoo is a small zoo that is very parent- and kid-friendly. It's also stroller-friendly. All paths go in a huge circle, making it very hard to get lost. There are more than 400 animals in this old oak forest along the Red Cedar River. Kids see pandas, wolves, kangaroos, lions, ostriches, rhinos, leopards, peacocks, and otters up close.

Bring your small children to Farmyard Encounters, a special section with a neat red barn, giant white silo, and little barns full of animals, including a yak and reindeer. Kids can feed the animals and sanitize their hands before and after. There's even a veterinary clinic where kids can peek into the window of its operating room.

Adjacent to the farm are pony rides. The weight limit is 100 pounds, and a child under two years of age must be accompanied by an adult. There are also camel rides for older children and adults.

The zoo gift shop sells a huge selection of animal-themed kits, books, clothes, school supplies, puzzles, and plush and rubber animals. Bring your camera; around the zoo are cutout images of animals for children to stick their heads through for a photo opportunity.

The zoo also offers family events year-round, such as Breakfast with the Animals, Boo at the Zoo, and Wonderland of Lights, plus birthday parties, overnights, scout badge programs, and camp.

Western Michigan

Go Box

6151 Portage Road
Portage 49002

866-524-7966 or 269-382-6555.
www.airzoo.org

Jan.–Mar.: 10–5 Mon.–Sat., noon–5 Sun.
Apr.–May & Sept.–Dec.: 10–5 Mon.–Fri.,
10–6 Sat., noon–6 Sun. June–Aug.: 10–6
Mon.–Sat., noon–6 Sun.

$19.50 adults, $15.50 ages 5–15, $17.50
seniors, free for children 4 & under.
Discounted fees for active or retired
military & their family.

Free on site

All ages

My Notes

Fun Food

The Kitty Hawk Café, on the museum's second level, gives you a bird's-eye view of the airplanes while you eat. It offers pizza, salads, sandwiches, hot dogs, hamburgers, bagels, and muffins, plus snacks and beverages.

Field Tip

Go on to the Air Zoo Annex only if your child is an airplane or history aficionado. It's filled with World War II planes and static historic readings and artifacts. At the back of the exhibit space is a C-47 transport aircraft that kids can enter.

Air Zoo

Bright, airy, and modern, the Air Zoo is both a theme park and a museum. While telling the story of flight and, more specifically, of World War II fliers and the NASA space program, it offers a Kids' Room, rides, a 4-D theater, space shuttle flight simulators, and more than 80 vintage aircraft.

The curving entrance, with its mural of a light blue sky and white clouds, makes you light-headed. Once inside the cavernous museum space, you'll see the beginning of another mural to your left, wrapping around the museum's perimeter to tell the story of flight from hot air balloons to space craft.

The walls of the Kids' Room are painted with fantastical flying beasts, scenes from Greek mythology, and flying machines. Here, kids can go on four small rides and play with airplanes and LEGOs on three tables.

Back in the exhibit space, you'll find rides for adults and older children taller than 36 and 48 inches. Look up and around you at the brightly colored World War II fighter jets—you'll see fighting roosters and planes painted with sharp white shark's teeth.

Put on black glasses and enter the Quonset hut for the 4-D movie. This patriotic 12-minute film fills you with the excitement of a bomber flying high above Nazi Germany who's hit with enemy fire and has to parachute out.

Hold on to your lunch at the flight simulator ride. Two people (at least 48 inches tall) go together, turning upside down and sideways. Then try the bouncy NASA Shuttle mission ride (for riders at least 42 inches tall).

The gift shop has a children's area selling an aviator teddy, model planes, wind socks, flying toys, books, posters, stickers, kaleidoscopes, marbles, gyroscopes, and other space and flying-related toys. The Air Zoo offers camps, school field trips, family and scout overnights, and special programs, such as the Family New Year's Eve Party.

Go Box

7400 Division Drive
Battle Creek 49014

269-979-1351. www.binderparkzoo.org

Last week in Apr.–first week in Oct.: 9–5
Mon.–Fri., 9–6 Sat., 11–6 Sun.

$11.95 adults, $9.95 ages 2–10, $10.95
seniors, free for children under 2. Strollers
& wheelchairs available for rental.

Free on site

All ages

My Notes

Fun Food

There are two choices for purchasing food at the zoo. Beulah's Restaurant, near the entrance, offers hamburgers, hot dogs, chili, salads, ice cream, and snacks. Kalahari Kitchen, in the African Village, offers hamburgers, hot dogs, chili, wraps, sandwiches, salads, and snacks. There are lots of picnic tables and shelters outside the zoo entrance.

Field Tip

Let the kids buy a souvenir at Zawadi Traders. They will feel like they've been to Africa. There are masks, musical instruments, plush animals, paint and play sets, jewelry, and dominoes, all with an African theme. Outside the store, they can sit and get their faces painted like an exotic animal or buy "pucker powder," sugary powdered candy.

Binder Park Zoo

The Binder Park Zoo offers a wonderfully creative experience for families and has placed its animals in two areas. Wild Africa is an imaginative experience that begins with a free Wilderness Tram ride to a site constructed to look like an African village. There are animals along the sides of an elevated looped boardwalk that's three-fourths of a mile long. The rest of the zoo includes the Children's Zoo, with domestic animals to pet and feed, a miniature train, and the Wildlife Discovery Theater. There is a restored carousel of hand-carved and hand-painted animals. Be sure to also check into the feeding times and Critter Chats posted at the entrance.

The African Safari is a reason to visit. The experience starts at the Wilderness Tram station, a breezy, covered area, festooned with African flags and sound effects of whistles, hoots, and drums. The tram offers a narration in English with Swahili words, making it seem like you are about to take a journey to a fictitious Zuri National Park in Africa. You emerge from the tram into the dusty center of a village, created like a stage set, surrounded by Zawadi Traders (an African gift shop), Kalahari Kitchen (a restaurant), and the beginning of the boardwalk loop.

The fun begins on the boardwalk. The first stop is the Safari office. There are more stops in huts or stations, great overlooks for animals grazing in natural habitats, animals to pet and feed up close, and easy-to-read information sheets. There are zebras, giraffes, ostriches, monkeys, vultures, cranes, antelopes, and birds. Highlights include giraffes you can pet and feed from a viewing window; the forest aviary, with its colorful birds; monkey valley, with white furry colobus monkeys hopping from tree to tree; and a little farm with chickens and Nubian goats.

The zoo also offers special events, such as family overnights, Halloween's Great ZooBoo, birthday parties, scout workshops, camp, and group visits.

 83

Go Box

415 Lake Boulevard
St. Joseph 49085

269-983-2543. www.curiouskidsmuseum.org

June 1–Labor Day: 10–5 Mon.–Sat., noon–5
Sun. Sept.–May 31: 10–5 Wed.–Sat., noon–5
Sun.

June 1–Labor Day: $6 ages 1 & up.
Sept.–May 31: $4 ages 1 & up.

Free on site

Infants–10 years

My Notes

Fun Food

Caffe Tosi (516 Pleasant St., 269-983-3354) offers an ambitious menu in a very bohemian atmosphere. Order coffee drinks, home-made breads, panini sandwiches, soups, pasta, breakfasts, and desserts cafeteria-style.

Field Tip

Kids will love exploring downtown St. Joseph. You can skip along the lake on a path adorned with outdoor sculpture. There are shops where you can buy fudge or ice cream cones, make your own stuffed animal, and paint plates and plaster shapes. At the South Bend Chocolate Company (300 State Street, 269-985-9866), you can buy chocolates by the pound and enjoy chocolate drinks and ice cream sundaes.

A carousel horse greets you on the porch of the brightly painted, two-story museum. Here, kids rule, and there are lots of rooms and nooks and crannies to explore.

Toddlers will love the Toddle Farm, with its little barn climber and slide, plush animals, and water table duck pond. Kids can put on costumes to become different animals, sit on a John Deere, play with giant blocks, and become mini-ballerinas at the baby ballet bar.

At the Geo Kids area, a volcano erupts, and kids can go down a slide, learn about dinosaurs, walk into an African safari room decorated with hanging vines, dress in bird costumes, and look at slides through microscopes.

In the Global Village's rural German classroom, kids can learn a little German and French and try on aprons and caps in the German home. There's a huge map of the world with buttons for kids to push to say where their family comes from.

Upstairs, imagination continues. Older children can try their hand at simple science displays, play music, learn about medicine, and pretend inside an ambulance.

The Space Room plays music from the film *2001: A Space Odyssey* and offers older kids a chance to sit inside a space capsule and fiddle with the controls.

A small gift shop sells T-shirts and sweatshirts, mood pens, bubbles, and dinosaurs. The museum offers scout programs, birthday parties, and school or group workshops.

Go Box

12350 James Street
Holland 49424

800-285-7177 or 616-396-1475.
www.dutchvillage.com

Last weekend in Apr.–first weekend in
Oct. Hours fluctuate but are generally
10–5:30 daily. Gift shop open year-
round, with varying hours.

$10 adults, $5 ages 4–15, $9 seniors

Free on site

All ages

My Notes

Fun Food

You can eat Dutch food at the Hungry Man Café on the grounds of
the theme park. Try saucijize broodjes (pigs in a blanket) or deep
fried croquettes of pork and beef. Or don't act adventurous and
have a salad or sandwich—ingredients are fresh and made to order.

Field Tip

For tulip growers and Dutch aficionados, Veldheer's Tulip Gardens
and DeKlomp Wooden Shoe and Delftware Factory (12755 Quincy
St., 616-399-1900) is two miles north of Dutch Village. Here, you
can watch Delft pottery being hand-painted and take tours of the
klompen factory. The tulip farms are spectacular in May.

The very best beach for small children in the Holland area is
Tunnel Park (www.holland.org), located west on Lakewood Blvd.
and then south on Lakeshore Dr. Entrance to the beach and Lake
Michigan is through a tunnel burrowed beneath a massive sand
dune. Kids can run through the tunnel, down the steps, and out onto
the open sand. Near the parking lot, there are a children's playground, a dune climb, and a dune stairway.

Dutch Village

It's only natural that Dutch Village looks commercial, sitting next to the highway and an outlet strip mall. But it has been lovingly put together to evoke a sense of Holland, and there are enough rides, demonstrations, and family activities to stay for several hours.

It pays to figure out your day in advance. Let the kids skip along the paths to Mother Hubbard's yellow wooden shoe slide. There's an antique carousel and, for older children and teens, a high-flying Dutch swing ride. Stop by the petting farm to feed a baby goat (25 cents for feed) and take him for a walk. Highlights are the witchcraft trial presentation (step on the scale to find out if you are a witch) and klompen dancers in the performance area (you can take a dance lesson after the performance). Watch Delft pottery being made; kids can color a Delft pattern on a paper plate.

Older children may enjoy the static exhibits of costumes and dolls in the small museums. Be sure to wander through the retail outlets to watch demonstrations of candle dipping and wooden shoe carving and to buy lots of Dutch goodies.

87

Go Box

1000 East Beltline Avenue NE
Grand Rapids 49525

888-957-1580.
www.meijergardens.org

9–5 Mon. & Wed.–Sat., 9–9 Tues.,
noon–5 Sun.

$12 adults, $6 ages 5–13,
$4 ages 3–4, $9 seniors,
free for children 2 & under

Free on site

All ages

My Notes

Fun Food

Taste of the Gardens Café, a cafeteria, offers sandwiches, wraps, salads, hot dishes, and snacks. Or treat the kids to ice cream at the old-fashioned Jersey Junction Ice Cream Parlor, located in East Grand Rapids (652 Croswell Ave. SE, 49506; 616-458-4107).

Field Tip

Cheer on the Whitecaps, a Class A affiliate in the Tigers Minor League. The Whitecaps play April through September in Fifth Third Ballpark, located in Comstock Park, seven miles north of Grand Rapids. For tickets, call 616-784-4131.

Frederik Meijer Gardens and Sculpture Park—Children's Garden

The five-acre Children's Garden in Meijer Gardens is the most wonderful and complete children's garden experience in Michigan. It's fully wheelchair accessible and offers 10 thematic play areas where children can explore and learn about Michigan nature. Be sure to pick up a map first. You can spend two hours or more here, so the bathrooms to the right of the entrance will come in handy.

Kids enter the garden through a *Secret Garden*–like door flanked by Marshall Frederick's sculpture of Momma and Baby Bear. Go through the Butterfly Maze and whisper to one another in the yellow and purple talking tubes. In a small alcove above the maze, you'll find storytelling, entertainment, or craft making several times a day during the summer.

Skip along the Sculpture Walk and notice a family of clowns juggling balls and a wolf family made with found objects. Follow the bricks to the center of the Labyrinth. Take the long elevated walk or climb up to the top of Treehouse Village, where you can look through telescopes placed at a kid's eye level, sit on giant bird eggs, and see pretend bugs clinging to the treehouse ceiling.

In the cool and calm Log Cabin, kids can play checkers and build things. The Rock Quarry offers them a giant sandbox with plastic toys for digging out buried fossils. They'll love getting wet and sailing toy boats in the Great Lakes Garden, the magnet for families on hot summer days. The Story-Telling Garden is full of floral sculptures of characters from nursery rhymes and other children's stories. In the Wooded Wetland, kids can look through viewers, and in the Kid-Sense Garden, a giant hand, eye, nose, ear, and tongue indicate how we use our senses to enjoy nature.

If you have the time, a stroller, and an intrepid child, you'll want to explore the entirety of Meijer Gardens—125 acres of wetlands, woodlands, meadows, and gardens, filled with more than 150 sculptures. Indoors, walk through the tropical, arid, Victorian, and carnivorous gardens and the sculpture gallery, with its multimedia presentation.

Meijer Gardens offers classes for families and children, story times, birthday parties, scout badge workshops, group and school tours, a butterfly show in March and April, and a concert series during the summer.

Go Box

303 Pearl Street NW
Grand Rapids 49504

616-254-0400.
www.fordlibrarymuseum.gov

9–5 daily

$7 adults, $3 ages 6–18,
$6 seniors & military,
free for children 5 & under

Free on site

10 & up

My Notes

Fun Food

The walk from the museum to downtown is less than a half mile. Kids will love walking over the Grand River. The upscale Sundance Grill and Bar (40 Pearl St. NW, 616-776-1616) serves breakfasts, sandwiches, burgers, salads, and lots of Southwest fare.

Field Tip

Park in the Ford Museum lot and walk across the street to visit the Van Andel Museum too.

The Ford Museum has one of the best gift shops around if you want your child to learn about American history and our presidents or their wives. There are books for all ages, decks of cards, candies, T-shirts, paper dolls, puzzles, and place mats. You'll also find an assortment of books about Michigan.

Gerald Ford Museum

President Gerald Ford is the only president we Michiganders can call our own, so it's fun to learn about him and visit his library museum. But most of the exhibits are about events that took place way before your kids were born and are basically static, except for two walk-in spaces, so the museum is only suitable for patient older elementary schoolchildren and younger history buffs.

But what fun it is to walk into those spaces! The first is a replica Oval Office. You've seen many in the movies, so this one won't be a surprise. What's fun is the audio of a typical day in the life of President Ford, with his voice, all his guests' voices, and the voice of his secretary. The second space is a replica Cabinet Room. You can sit at the long oval table and play with a computer program about President Ford's pardon of President Nixon.

Kids may find the multimedia exhibit of the life and times of President Ford interesting, especially if they watch reruns of *That '70s Show*. There are display cases full of hippie clothing and movie posters, and three video screens flash telecasts from the times, showing clips of the assassinations of Martin Luther King Jr. and Bobby Kennedy, Kent State, the Chicago Seven Trial, Patricia Hearst, and Kissinger winning the Nobel Peace Prize.

You can trace Michigan's favorite son from birth to his accidental ascent to the presidency and learn about his leadership style and what took place during his presidency. He pardoned Nixon, ended the Vietnam War, and took part in shuttle diplomacy between Israel and Egypt. You'll also learn about his wife, Betty, and his children and see gifts that were given to him. Since President Ford was buried on the grounds of the museum, you can go out to the grave to pay your respects.

Go Box

22 Sheldon Avenue NE
Grand Rapids 49503

616-235-4726. www.grcm.org

9:30–5 Tues., Wed., Fri., & Sat.;
9:30–8 Thurs.; noon–5 Sun.;
9:30–5 Mon. during summer

$5 ages 2 & up, free for under 2.
Family night, 5–8 Thurs., $1/person,
children under 2 are free.

Use metered street parking

Infants–10 years

My Notes

Fun Food

Around the corner from the museum is the upscale coffee shop and restaurant Café Solace (40 Monroe Center, 616-632-2233). You can sit up high on stools and swing your legs or sit in comfy chairs and order smoothies, coffee drinks, omelets, sandwiches, wraps, and salads.

Field Tip

Be sure to go to Calder Plaza, on Ottawa between Michigan and Lyon NW, to see *La Vitesse*, a large red-orange outdoor sculpture by Alexander Calder. Kids will love touching it and running around it and through it.

Grand Rapids Children's Museum

This is hands down the best children's museum in Michigan, with all the types of exhibits found in children's museums around Michigan and then more. Bright, gaily colored banners sporting the words "Play, Create, Learn," fly from the second story of this full city-block museum. There is even a Kids' Entrance through a small door into the two-story playland.

Pick up a map or just wander through the two stories. The play stations on the first level include a sandbox with colorful toys; a mom-and-pop grocery store complete with carts and fake food; a campfire to read next to; a construction site with tools and dress-up hard hats and tool belts; Grandma's Bakery, with a cash register and fake pastries; and a puppet theater and amphitheater, with clothes for dressing up and putting on a show or becoming a weather reporter. There is also a Wee Discover Room just for children under 5, with soft blocks and creative toys.

Upstairs you'll find the traveling exhibit, plus a permanent tree house where kids can play, crawl, and slide; a giant bubble hoop for four kids at a time; a shape puzzle table; a play restaurant kitchen; a play bank with drive-in window and ATM machine; a craft table full of yarn, glue, and drawing materials; a pretend garden with vegetables to harvest; a beehive area with real honeycomb, bee costumes, and white veiled beekeepers' hats.

The museum has a wonderful gift shop, with snacks, books, plush toys, puppets, T-shirts, hats, and educational and craft kits.

Go Box

1300 West Fulton
Grand Rapids 49504

616-336-4300.
www.johnballzoosociety.org

Sat. after Mother's Day–Mon. after Labor Day:
9–6 daily. Rest of year: 10–4. Closed December 25.

Daily Apr.–Oct. & weekends Nov. &
Mar.: $6 adults, $4 ages 4–13, $4.50
seniors, free for children 3 & under.
Free Dec.–Feb. Fee for camel rides
and swan paddleboats. Strollers are
available for rental.

Free on site

All ages

My Notes

Fun Food

During the summer, there are two zoo restaurants, plus concessions around the zoo and picnic tables near the Sting Ray Lagoon and Treasures of the Tropics. The zoo restaurants sell chicken sandwiches, pizza, hot dogs and hamburgers, ice cream, and other snacks.

Field Tip

During May through October, cool off at Millennium Park (616-336-3697, www.millennium-park.org), which includes a water park with giant sprays, water cannons, and dumping buckets and a six-acre beach with a swimming lake.

John Ball Zoo

The John Ball Zoo is small enough that you can stroll along the oblong path and see all the exhibits and most of the animals in two or three hours. In a shorter visit, you can concentrate on one or two highlights. Many exhibits are at kids' eye level, close to the path and very accessible.

Among the many highlights are the small indoor exhibit of cnidarians (pronounced ny-dare-ee-uhns)—translucent jellyfish and amoeba-like Medusas, all with no bones, blood, or brains—and the aquarium, where you'll see waterfalls, waves, penguins, colorful fish, coral, sharks, and starfish. In the summer, a tank of stingrays is stationed outside the aquarium; for a small fee, you can touch their velvety bodies.

There's a petting corral for small children, and there are camel rides for bigger children. In the Tropical World reptile house, you can see bats, flying squirrels, scorpions, iguanas, crocodiles, snakes, and a Komodo dragon. There are lots of monkeys in Mokomboso Valley, where an elevated walkway overlooks a natural habitat full of chimpanzees and other species.

Be sure to ask at the entrance about special events and times for keeper talks and live bird shows. The gift shop sells a great variety of plastic animals and puzzles, backpacks, clothes, plush toys, purses, stickers, and masks—all with an animal theme. The zoo hosts birthday parties, overnights, and school and group visits.

Go Box

7000 Westnedge Avenue
Kalamazoo 49009

269-381-1574.
www.NatureCenter.org

9–5 Mon.–Sat., 1–5 Sun.

$6 adults, $4 ages 4–13, $5 seniors, free for children 3 & under

Free on site

All ages

My Notes

Fun Food

It's all trains all the time at the Club Car Restaurant (6225 West D Avenue, 269-342-8087). After a train crossing sign greets you at the front door, you step into railroad cars decorated to the hilt with train photos, signs, memorabilia, and luggage. A small gift shop sells Thomas the Tank Engine books; mini-trains; engineer caps; and train books, erasers, pencils, and banks. Waitresses dressed as train engineers give kids coloring sheets, crayons, and plastic train whistles.

Field Tip

Follow M-43 west only 23 miles and you'll come to South Haven, a charming town with a great downtown and lots of beaches. Visit around the end of July or beginning of August to find a ton of blueberry farms with crops ripe for the picking. South Haven's Blueberry Festival is the second week of August.

Kalamazoo Nature Center

The Kalamazoo Nature Center was created for kids. From the parking lot, they can fly down the winding ramp and skip across the wooden plank bridge into the spacious and airy building. Once inside, there are live and stuffed animals and vegetation displays, a parent-child space, a rain forest room, and a special exhibit downstairs.

Kids can see real frogs, turtles, and fish in an aquarium; they can also press buttons and learn to identify chirping, buzzing, and trilling with the right animal. In a special area with a large window onto the outdoors, small children can relax on couches and watch birds near a bird feeder or read nature books and magazines with their parents; they can put on a puppet show in the small puppet theater, play with nature puzzles, or look at feathers or leaves under a microscope.

In the atrium's two-story rain forest, kids can see a giant tree with hanging vines; feel the warmth; see birds, frogs, and purple flowers; and hear water dripping. The downstairs exhibit space offers them a whimsical space to explore bugs or other nature topics.

Items in the gift shop help kids explore nature. Rocks, whirligigs, marbles, finger puppets, books, bug and dinosaur kits, plush toys, and magnifying bug viewers are on sale. The Nature Center offers camps, classes, scout badge workshops, overnights, birthday parties, nature preschool, and special family events, such as March's Maple Syrup Festival and December's Holidays at the Homestead. During the summer, don't miss the outdoor hummingbird and butterfly garden.

Go Box

230 North Rose Street
Kalamazoo 49003

800-772-3370 or 269-373-7990.
www.kalamazoomuseum.org

Museum: 9–5 Mon.–Sat., 1–5 Sun.
Children's Landscape: 9–3
Mon.–Fri., 9–5 Sat., 1–5 Sun.

Free

Use spaces on nearby streets

All ages

My Notes

Fun Food

The downtown area near the museum is full of restaurant choices. My favorite is Food Dance (401 E. Michigan Ave., 269-382-1888), a whimsical restaurant filled with wall paintings of sprites, giant asparagus stalks, and other vegetables. It's a great place to play "I Spy" while waiting for upscale sandwiches, hamburgers, soups, and salads.

Field Tip

The Kalamazoo Art Museum (314 S. Park St., 269-349-7775, www.kiarts .org), a short walk away, is small enough for a quick walk through the galleries. The Artworks Gallery on the bottom level is set up for kids. In each of eight displays, you are shown a famous artist's work and given suggestions for creating your own artwork using the artist's style. A gift shop offers great toys, dolls, books, and kits for kids.

Kalamazoo Valley Museum

There's something for everyone at the modern, three-floor Kalamazoo Valley Museum—the special preschool Children's Landscape, a mummy exhibit, history and science displays, a simulated space mission ride, a planetarium, and a theater series.

Children's Landscape is a wonderful indoor playground for ages 5 and under. Kids can burn off steam on a climber, create crafts, play with a dollhouse, ride a bus, try on costumes, and build with giant LEGO blocks. There are free entertainers the first Saturday of each month and free preschool art, stories, music, science, or math programming Monday through Saturday year-round.

Museum highlights include the Mysteries of the Mummy, a high-tech exhibit of two mummies—human and animal. Science in Motion offers lots of hands-on displays where kids can play and learn. Families can build a magnetic sculpture or race car and learn about their body in motion by dancing. The second-floor On the Trail of History is slated for renovation and expected to reopen with many more high-tech, hands-on displays.

There are special monthly events, planetarium shows, and Saturday family performances and movie matinees. Check for times on the Web. The museum also offers scout and school programs.

Go Box

4750 Whitehall Road
Muskegon 49445

231-766-3377.
www.miadventure.com

Hours fluctuate all summer. In general, both the amusement park and WildWater Adventure are open Mem. Day–Labor Day: the amusement park, 11–9 daily; WildWater Adventure, noon–7 daily. The amusement park is open some weekend dates before Mem. Day & after Labor Day.

$24 adults & children (includes WildWater Adventure and most amusement park rides—except Go-Karts & RipCord), free for children 2 & under. For group rates or season pass, call 231-766-9959.

$7/car

All ages

Fun Food

There are concession stands and restaurants all over the park, where you can find pizza, hot dogs, hamburgers, ice cream, snacks, and beverages. Nonpark food and beverages, picnic baskets, and coolers are not permitted in the park.

Field Tip

Plan on a full day at Michigan's Adventure. Be prepared. Bring towels and swimsuits for the water park, plus sunscreen, caps, and sunglasses. You need to wear shoes, shirts, and pants/shorts at the amusement park. Plan to change out of wet clothes or into swimsuits at some time during the day. It pays to rent your lockers when you arrive.

My Notes

Michigan's Adventure Amusement Park

Join costumed Snoopy and other Charlie Brown characters at Michigan's only amusement park. It's clean, safe, and busy, with more than 50 rides and a water park. Each ride is rated, going from low to aggressive thrill. For small children, there are approximately 14 rides rated low to mild thrill in the amusement park and 3 rides rated low thrill in the water park.

You'll find family rides (the Carousel, Timbertown Railway, Winky the Whale, and the Giant Gondola Wheel) and rides for small kids on their own (the Elephants, the Airplanes, and the Kiddie Cars). For teens, there are six roller coasters, including Shivering Timbers, which soars and plunges for over a mile, climbing 125 feet and then zooming to 65 miles per hour.

The park has thought of everything from changing rooms, lockers, and showers (you need to wear a swimsuit to go into the water park) to rentals of wagons, strollers, wheelchairs, and inner tubes. At the wave pool, you can rent a cabana that will accommodate up to 8 people for $50. 231-766-9959.

Go Box

6495 Blue Star Highway
Saugatuck 49453

269-857-2253.
www.saugatuckduneride.com

Apr.–June & Sept.–Oct.: 10–5:30 Mon.–Sat.,
noon–5:30 Sun. July–Labor Day weekend:
10–7:30 Mon.–Sat., noon–7:30 Sun.

$15 adults, $10 ages 3–10, free for
children under 3. Cash only.

Free on site

6 & up

My Notes

Fun Food

Drive into Saugatuck for food. There are many fudge and ice cream shops in the shopping district. For relaxing in a booth with specialty pizza and pick-your-own toppings, go to Marro's Italian Restaurant (147 Water St., 269-857-4248).

Field Tip

There are several beaches near Saugatuck, most notably Oval Beach on Lake Michigan, a sandy family-friendly beach with all the amenities. During the summer season, Interurban Bus Service will take you out to Oval Beach. Call and reserve it (269-857-1418); they will pick you up at any location in the area.

Saugatuck Dune Rides

This is one of those experiences that your kids will love and beg you to do again next summer. The scare level is high as you approach the ramshackle wooden house, home to Dune Schooner Rides in Saugatuck. A bunch of signs on the fence read: "Danger," "Asian Bats," "Do Not Feed!" Look closely and you'll see a couple of baseball bats in a case, presumably signed by Japanese players. That joke alone gives you a clue that this dune ride is going to be more fun than fear.

There is a method to choosing your seat in the five-row, open-air jeep. If you are squeamish or don't like being jostled, bumped, and tossed about, don't sit on the ends of a row; sit in the middle of a row in the middle of the jeep. The driver sits in the first row with two guests, usually adventure-seeking types. Those same types whoop it up in the last row and on the sides. In between are the more placid riders.

Then comes the fun, a 35-minute ride, going up and around and over lots of bumps and endless trails of sand, turning suddenly, and going very quickly while the driver makes lots of quips and jokes as he drives, such as "The funny part is you guys think I work here" and "It only hurts once when you're hit by a tree." You might be lucky and see Lake Michigan or a deer. Take my word for it, the ride ends too soon.

Go Box

Great Lakes Naval Memorial & Museum
1346 Bluff Street
Muskegon 49441

231-755-1230.
www.glnmm.org

Apr. & Oct.: 10–5:30 Sat. & Sun. May & Sept.:
1–5 Mon.–Fri., 10–5:30 Sat. & Sun. June–Aug.:
10–5:30 daily. Tour both ships in approximately
90 mins.

$8 ages 19–61, $7 students ages 12–18 & seniors,
$6 ages 5–11; free for 4 & under, active military per-
sonnel, & World War II submarine veterans.
Admission includes tour of USS *Silversides* &
USCGC *McLane*. Reservations needed for groups.

Free on site

6 & up

My Notes

Fun Food

Rafferty's (730 Terrace Point Blvd., 231-722-4461) overlooks the marina on Muskegon Lake. You can eat roll-up sandwiches, salads, and burgers outdoors on the terrace.

Field Tip

Just 10 miles south of the USS *Silversides,* along the shore of Lake Michigan, you'll find P. J. Hoffmaster State Park (6585 Lake Harbor Road, Muskegon). This state park offers three miles of sandy beach, the E. Genevieve Gillette Sand Dune Visitor Center (231-798-3573), and a bird's-eye view of the water after climbing (count 'em!) 150 steps on the top of a dune overlook.

USS Silversides

Patient children who have grown up with stories of the glories of war will enjoy touring this submarine, launched in 1941. Commissioned after Pearl Harbor, the USS *Silversides* performed 14 war patrols, sinking 30 and damaging 16 Japanese ships. Sustaining only one fatality, it earned the title "Luckiest of the Fleet."

A tour guide takes you all over the submarine, explaining how everything worked. Below deck, you see how both the enlisted men and the officers slept intertwined with torpedoes. The men slept, ate, worked, used the toilet, and showered in these cramped quarters with narrow passageways. The tour guide helps you imagine how the smells and claustrophobia intensified during a 52-day patrol.

You can also tour the smaller 1927 USCGC *McLane*, a Coast Guard rum chaser during Prohibition. There's a great military gift shop in the museum selling space magnets, water guns, model World War II submarines, puzzles, decals, T-shirts, caps, and Frisbees. Scouts can arrange sleepovers in the submarine.

Go Box

272 Pearl Street NW
Grand Rapids 49504

616-456-3977.
www.grmuseum.org

9–4 Mon.–Fri., 10–4 Sat.,
noon–4 Sun.

$8 adults, $3 ages 3–17, $7
seniors, free for children
under 3. Carousel rides: $1.

Free in the Gerald Ford
Museum lot

2 & up

My Notes

Fun Food

Eat at the second-floor Museum Café and enjoy breakfast food, cheese-burgers, sandwiches, salads, soups, and desserts. Or go to San Chez, a Tapas Bistro (38 W. Fulton, 616-774-8272), a lively, colorful two-story restaurant where all the food is served as hors d'oeuvres on small plates.

Field Tip

The museum's gift shop is huge and offers instruments and CDs, kits, books, castles, alphabet erasers, candles, space food, gems, gummy mummies, beads, sticker and coloring books, posters, and loads of Egyptian merchandise. The museum also runs summer camps, birthday parties, classes, field trips, and scout workshops. When entering the museum, ask for the schedule of organ concerts, laser light shows, and planetarium shows in the Roger B. Chaffee Planetarium (616-456-3977).

Leave time for the new Grand Rapids Art Museum (101 Monroe Center, 616-831-6000, www.gramonline.org), scheduled to open in the fall of 2007. It will include a children's gallery and look onto a new urban park.

This museum has so many exhibits and displays that it's hard to know what to do first. Start at the restored 1928 Spillman carousel and take the five-minute ride on hand-painted animals. Parents and grandparents can sit on rockers and watch as the kids go round and round. Explore the Streets of Old Grand Rapids and listen for voices of the past. You'll hear immigrants and the conductor in the train waiting room and a newspaper boy hawking the *Herald* on the street. Peek into old storefronts, sit on an early bicycle and Model T, and play with an old-fashioned phone.

On the second level, you learn about Grand Rapids as Furniture City and play with an iron, washboard, and rug beater in the Grand Rapids Cleans Up display. There are Western and non-Western instruments in a small music exhibit, where kids make their own music by plucking, striking, bowing, and blowing.

The third floor offers many press-and-learn displays—about baby animals, preserved animals, fish, and Michigan environments. Highlights include the Egyptian room, where a mummy lies and a skull is reconstructed, and the Anishinabek display, where you can sit on a couch and watch a sensitive video about Michigan's first people—their beliefs, values, and art. All around are A–Z displays about Grand Rapids' past, natural science, and history. Older children should pick up a scavenger hunt form at the entrance.

Go Box

1 Lincoln Avenue
Holland

616-355-1030.
www.windmillisland.org

Next-to-last weekend in Apr.–first weekend in Oct.: 10–5 daily. During tulip time
(first and second Sat. in May): 9–6 daily.

$7 adults, $4 ages 5–15

Free on site

Infants–10 years

My Notes

Fun Food

Bring a picnic and supplement with drinks and snacks. There are picnic tables all over. Or drive into downtown Holland, where there are lots of restaurants. Kids will love Froggy's (80 E. 8th St., 616-546-FROG [3764]), where the specialties are chili dogs, hamburgers, and hand-cut french fries and everything is served in baskets.

Field Tip

During Tulip Time, Holland is ablaze with millions of tulips and celebrates its Dutch heritage with klompen dancers, street concerts, an arts and crafts fair, parades, a carnival, and fireworks. For more information, call Tulip Time Festival, Inc. (800-822-2770) or visit www.tuliptime.com.

Downtown Holland is fun to stroll through. You'll find upscale art galleries; book, music, hobby, and clothing stores; fudge, ice cream, and coffee shops; and lots of restaurants. From mid-June through August, enjoy street performers throughout the downtown area from 5:30 to 8 on Thursdays. Older children will benefit from a scavenger hunt through the historic displays at the Holland Museum (31 W. 10th St., 888-200-9123, www.hollandmuseum.org). Pick up an "I Spy Adventure" activity at the entrance desk.

Windmill Island

Windmill Island is the next best thing to visiting Holland with your family. Quiet and pleasant, it has well-kept grassy lawns, colorful flower borders, hanging flower baskets, white picket fences, canals, Dutch architecture, and De Zwaan, the 200-year-old windmill situated on the banks of the Macatawa River.

Kids will love watching the klompen dancers, boys and girls dressed in Dutch folk costumes and wooden shoes. Their spirited dancing takes place in front of the windmill. Kids can try on wooden shoes and clothes and take a tour up through the windmill, peeking out the windows to the ground far below and learning all sorts of interesting facts, such as the shoe on the rope hanging in the center of the mill's ground floor operated as a telephone for the miller who was working on the top floors.

Kids can ride a colorful carousel, get friendly with cows and other domesticated animals, traipse over a bridge, listen to a calliope organ, and, in the Dutch marketplace, watch candle dipping and buy Dutch souvenirs and treats.

Northern Michigan
& the Upper Peninsula

Go Box

Located at the base of the Mackinac Bridge. Take exit 339 from I-75 or take Huron Street west along the water in downtown Mackinaw City.

231-436-4100.
www.mackinacparks.com

May 7–June 8 & Aug. 25–Oct. 7: 9–4 daily (open until 6 on Labor Day weekend). June 9–Aug. 25: 9–6 daily.

$10 adults, $6 ages 6–17, free for children 5 & under. If you are going to Mackinac Island, think about the combo ticket—three daily admissions for a discounted fee includes Colonial Michilimackinac, Historic Mill Creek, Old Mackinac Point Lighthouse, or Mackinac Island's Fort Mackinaw.

Free on site

3 & up

My Notes

Fun Food

Be sure to have some pasties, the Upper Peninsula specialty, at the Mackinaw Pastie & Cookie Co., with two locations (516 S. Huron, 231-436-5113; 117 W. Jamet, 231-436-8202). They serve up beef, chicken, and vegetable and cheese pasties with special toppings—cheddar and mozzarella cheese; sour cream; or taco, marinara, or stroganoff sauces. Take a tip from me—they are better without the sauces. The city's shopping areas have an abundance of fudge, candy, and ice cream shops.

Field Tip

Older children will enjoy visiting Old Mackinac Point Lighthouse (open daily, mid-May–early Oct.). You must be four feet tall to go to the top. Walk up the winding staircase to the top floor for a view of the bridge and the lake and learn, from a costumed docent, about how the lighthouse tried to keep ships from destruction from 1892 to 1957. Another option is Historic Mill Creek, where there are sawmill demonstrations and lots of nature trails.

Colonial Michilimackinac

Start in the Colonial Michilimackinac Visitor's Center and watch the 13-minute movie about the first peoples to live and work in this area—Native Americans, French fur traders (or Voyageurs), and missionaries. Learn about the British story after the French and Indian War and Pontiac's Rebellion, which led to the Native American assault on the fort. It becomes quickly obvious that the fort you are about to walk around is just a reconstructed reproduction of the fort that was once on Mackinac Island.

Once inside the fort, kids can peak into homes, offices, and a church and walk along the ramparts around the fort's perimeter, high enough to see Lake Michigan and the Mackinac Bridge. They can pose next to a dug-out Voyageur canoe and sit on benches on the parade ground as British soldiers, wearing red woolen greatcoats, black felt tricornered hats, white breeches and tights, and button-up boots, demonstrate marching and then firing cannons over the straits. Other demonstrations include children's games, a French Colonial wedding and dance, and the arrival of the Voyageurs.

It's hard not becoming distracted in the gift shop, one of the largest you will see in this area. It's full of things kids love, including books about Voyageurs, Native Americans and their legends, colonial flags, and the American Revolution; paraphernalia for birding and nature collecting for kids; tricornered hats; binoculars; Jacob's ladders, marbles, and other early games; and plush animals and rag dolls.

Go Box

4216 Ranger Road
Grayling 49738

517-348-7068.
www.michigan.gov/loggingmuseum

May 1–25 & Sept. 5–Oct. 31: 9–4 daily. May 26–Sept. 4: 9–7 daily.

Free

Daily vehicle pass: $6 resident, $8 nonresident

4 & up

My Notes

Fun Food

Go to Goodale's Bakery, located eight miles south of Hartwick Pines, on the south end of town (500 Norway St., 989-348-8682), for local flavor—fresh beef and chicken pasties, deli sandwiches, soups, macaroni & cheese, sweets, pastries, and freshly baked breads. Their apple cinnamon bread is a specialty. For a treat, try their cinnamon elephant ears.

For hand-dipped ice cream, you can't beat Wimpy's (6415 W. M-72, 989-344-1918). They also sell coneys, burgers, cheese fries, hot dogs, and sloppy joes. Sit outside at a pastel-painted picnic table.

Field Tip

Just 21 miles south of Hartwick Pines is the Civilian Conservation Corps Museum (11747 N. Higgins Lake Dr., Roscommon 48653; 517-373-3559; www.michigan.gov/cccmuseum), dedicated to the work during the Depression of more than 100,000 men who were given jobs reinvigorating Michigan's state parks.

Hartwick Pines State Park

Hartwick Pines is more than a leisurely walk in the quiet, sweet-smelling virgin white pine forest. With nearly 10,000 acres, it is the biggest state park in the Lower Peninsula. The Michigan Forest Visitor Center is the Michigan forest industry's official interpretive center, offering hands-on displays, dioramas, and artifacts from the rustic logging era of the late 1800s to today's modern, high-tech forestry industries. Within the center is an auditorium featuring a 14-minute multi-image slide program about Michigan's forests.

A paved trail through the forest leads to the 155-foot-tall Monarch, the tallest white pine in the grove, at least 300 years old. The trail also takes you to the lumber camp, the best part for kids. See where the "shanty boys" ate, slept, worked, and played. There is a great display showing a lumberman's daily breakfast. It seems like only Paul Bunyan could put away so much flapjacks, bacon, potatoes, beans, bread, and tin mugs of coffee. Walk into a bunk to see their beds, their red flannel long johns and dirty socks hanging to dry on makeshift laundry lines. Outside are huge pieces of historical lumbering equipment.

Back in the gift shop, you'll find a huge selection of toys and gifts that tell the story of Michigan history. On several summer weekends, the camp comes alive. The steam engine from the working sawmill is fired up to cut lumber, and costumed presenters demonstrate blacksmithing and carving.

Go Box

Mackinac Island

800-454-5227.
www.mackinac.com/index.html.
Fort Mackinac, 231-436-4100.

Fort Mackinac: mid-June–Aug., 9:30–8 daily; first week in May–mid-June and after Labor Day weekend–first week in Oct., 9:30–4:30 daily.

Fort Mackinac: $10.00 adults, $6 ages 6–17, free for 5 & under

No cars allowed on the island

All ages

My Notes

Fun Food

Eat outdoors high up on the ramparts at the fort's Tea Room Restaurant (906-847-3331, ext. 619) and have a bird's-eye view of the lake and bridge. If you're quiet, you'll hear gulls calling, birds chirping, and blasts from the ferries and cannons. In town, travel back to the mid-19th century and have an old-fashioned meal at the Yankee Rebel Tavern (906-847-6249). Eat outdoors in the lovely gardens of Hotel Iroquois (906-847-3321 Apr.–Oct., 616-247-5675 Nov.–mid-Apr.). Visit the Grand Hotel (800-333-7263) and have afternoon tea.

Field Tip

There are three ferry companies, with departures from Mackinaw City and St. Ignace pretty much every hour 7:30–9:30 daily June–Labor Day, less often May–October. The catamarans take you to the island in about 15 minutes.

Shepler's Mackinac Island Ferry, 800-828-6157 or 231-436-5023. www.sheplers ferry.com
Arnold Line, 800-542-8528 or 906-847-3351. www.arnoldline.com
Star Line Mackinac Island Ferry, 800-638-9892 or 906-643-7635. www.mackinac ferry.com

Mackinac Island

In the high summer season, Mackinac Island is noisy and crowded. Throngs of tourists walk from fudge shop to T-shirt shop along Main Street, and you need to keep your eyes open for horses and buggies—and horse plop. For a stay without crowds, think about visiting in late May, early June, or early fall.

By far, families will find bicycling around the island and visiting the fort well worth their time. Treat your kids to a little fudge so they can call each other "Fudgies," the name locals give to all visitors.

At Fort Mackinac, kids watch demonstrations of music and dance, rifle and cannon firing, military music, and dramatic reenactments. In Kids' Quarters, four rooms with experiential, hands-on displays, kids can try on period clothes, use a butter churn and washboard, play a giant fife, pose for a Civil War photo, learn how to use Morse code, and drill with a rifle.

Rent bicycles at a number of outlets dotting Main Street. Most rent side trailers for small children, some have bikes with training wheels, and all give you helmets. Most charge approximately $4/hour, with a $15 deposit for the bicycle (more for a bike with a trailer).

The Original Butterfly House is located just five minutes away from downtown and offers kids an up-close experience with butterflies. There are also bug exhibits, interactive displays, and reptiles in their natural habitats (10–7 daily Mem. Day–Labor Day; closes one hour earlier the rest of the year, 906-847-3972).

Go Box

Follow signs along Lake Superior shoreline to Munising City Pier

800-650-2379 or 906-387-2379. www.picturedrocks.com

Hours vary throughout the summer. Cruise runs Mem. Day weekend–mid-Oct., weather permitting. July–mid-Aug. 9, 11, noon, 1, 3, & 5.

$30 adults, $13 ages 6–12, free for children 5 & under

Free on site

6 & up

My Notes

Fun Food

Ron and Mary operate the Munising Bakery (115 W. Superior St., 906-387-2148), just two streets from the Pictured Rocks Boat Tour office. Everything is homemade—breakfast foods, doughnuts, sandwiches, pasties, and soups. Eat and browse through books at a comfortable coffee shop, Falling Rock Café and Bookstore (104 E. Munising Ave., 906-387-3008). They sell both used and new books and a kids' Nature Journal Kit—Artist Field Pack, which includes watercolors, colored pencils, and a journal.

Field Tip

If your kids like boat rides and are game for an additional one, the Glass Bottom Boat Shipwreck Tour (Mem. Day–mid-Oct., 906-387-4477, www.shipwrecktours .com) will show them many mysterious underwater shipwrecks in the Alger Underwater Preserve. The narrated tour takes you along the Grand Island's painted rock face and is a pleasant way to spend two hours in the sun. However, to see the shipwrecks, you must look downward into the glass viewing well in the bottom of the boat, which might make some people feel nauseous.

Before visiting the national lakeshore, have your children, grades K–6, sign up to become WebRangers (www.nps.gov/webrangers), Junior Rangers of the National Park Service. You'll receive a free membership card, and at each national park visitor center (Pictured Rocks and Sleeping Bear Dunes are Michigan's two national parks), you'll get special passport stamps and find games to play. Ask at the visitor centers for the Junior Rangers activity book.

Pictured Rocks National Lakeshore Boat Cruise

You can go hiking, kayaking, and camping in the area of Pictured Rocks National Lakeshore, but the best way for families to see the rock formations and the striated colors is to take the boat cruise. Eat before or bring along a cooler of sandwiches and snacks. The boat only sells snacks and beverages. Bring drawing paper, books, or small toys for the kids. It takes 30 minutes to cruise out to the rocky area.

The two-and-a-half-hour, 30-mile round-trip cruise is glorious in sunny weather. (Skip the cruise in rainy and cold weather, unless you enjoy being seasick.) Slather on your sunscreen, wear your cap, and soak in the rays on the top deck, listening to the captain narrate. Learn about Lake Superior (it's the largest freshwater lake in the world), and see the effects of glaciers and natural springs. Learn what minerals have created the rocks' different colors: iron creates red, brown, and purple; calcium creates white; copper makes blue and green; magnesium makes black.

Patient children are rewarded with 15 miles of spectacular multicolored sandstone cliffs that rise more than 100 feet out of Lake Superior, plus arches and unusual rock formations with such names as Indian Face, Indian Drum, the Pirate, Chapel Cove, and Miner's Castle. Kids can also explore the captain's cockpit, feed crumbs to the seagulls, and pose for photos.

Stop in one of the visitor centers before the boat cruise. You'll find displays, a gift shop, and rangers who are happy to tell you about driving and hiking routes and to give you maps and times of special events. The two main centers are located at either end of the park. Pictured Rocks/Hiawatha National Forest Interagency Visitor Center (400 E. Munising Ave., junction of M-28 and H-58; 906-387-3700) is open mid-May through mid-October. Grand Sable Visitor Center (E21090 County Road H-58, one mile west of Grand Marais; 906-494-2660) is open Labor Day weekend through the end of September.

Munising Falls Interpretive Center (1505 Sand Point Rd., 906-387-4310) has brochures, information, and exhibits on iron making, logging, wildlife, and how the cliffs were formed.

For information on the national lakeshore, visit www.nps.gov/piro.

119

Go Box

18335 North Whitefish Point Road
Paradise 49768

Administration office, 800-635-1742;
museum, May 1–Oct. 31, 888-492-
3747. www.shipwreckmuseum.com

May 1–Oct. 31, 10–6

$28/family, $10 adults, $7 ages 6–17,
free for children 5 & under

Free on site

6 & up

My Notes

Fun Food

Little Falls Inn Restaurant (east side of M-123, downtown Paradise; 906-492-3529), a rustic log building, is a good choice for basic food and is connected to an ice cream parlor.

For dense, chewy bread, baked the old-fashioned way in a brick oven, visit North Star Bakery (along M-123, between Newbery and Paradise; 906-658-3537), open June through October.

Field Tip

Climb down the wooden stairs at the far side of the museum to Lake Superior, which gets colder and more feisty as the summer season wanes. Let the kids dip their bare feet in Lake Superior's cool waves. Wander along the coastline and collect stones.

Shipwreck Museum and Whitefish Point

After watching the short movie about the shipwreck of the *Edmund Fitzgerald* and going through the museum's displays, your kids will realize why Lake Superior is the most treacherous of the Great Lakes. More than 30,000 people have died from shipwrecks at Whitefish Point, from the first recorded in 1679 to the present.

The museum tells the story of Lake Superior from the Native Americans and French trappers to the days of the U.S. Lighthouse Service and the first recorded shipwrecks. Most of the artifacts were found deep beneath the water, in wrecks. Kids listening carefully will hear seagulls, foghorns, and Gordon Lightfoot's "Wreck of the Edmund Fitzgerald" playing softly in the background.

The gift shop sells lots of nautical-themed toys and gifts, from small lighthouses to children's Great Lakes history books, small boats, sailors' whistles, and kits to learn how to make sailor's knots or build a ship in a bottle.

My Notes

Fun Food

Be sure to treat the kids to homemade ice cream cones, cookies, muffins, or deli sandwiches at the Old Mission General Store (18250 Mission Rd., Old Mission 49686; 231-223-4310). Opened in 1830, the store still runs a post office and offers penny candy, dried cherries, ginger snaps, and pickles. Old farm tools hang on the walls and from the ceiling, along with baskets, long johns, and old-fashioned phones.

Back in Traverse City, don't miss Sledder's Family Tavern (717 Randolph St., 231-947-9213). It was established in 1882 and serves great burgers, salads, and sandwiches. Notice the original ceiling and 21-foot bar—it is solid mahogany with a cherry wood side. Sit in the old section, among the funny signage and moose heads. If you kiss a moose head, your server will ring a bell.

If you go to the Sleeping Bear Point Maritime Museum, stop for lunch in Glen Arbor, a sleepy summer tourist town. The upscale Pinecone Grill (6584 Western Ave., 49636; 231-334-3555) offers sandwiches, wraps, soups, and salads.

Field Tip

Visit the small Dennos Museum Center (1701 E. Front St., Traverse City 49686; 231-995-1055). Play with an antigravitational mirror, holograms, and interactive sound sculpture. The gift shop sells clay sets, puppets, toys, and more.

The Sleeping Bear Point Maritime Museum has a red barn with blacksmith demonstrations and a boathouse lifesaving station where demonstrations of rescue equipment show how the U.S. Life Saving Service tried to save shipwreck victims. Get information from park headquarters on Front St. (231-326-5134).

Here you'll find sand and more sand, a desert of sand, ripples of thick sand for as far as you can see. Kids will love the sand dunes, dream about the Dune Climb, and bug you to visit again next summer, so first visit when they are old enough (and you spry enough) to climb at least partway up the side of the large 150-foot-tall dune at the Dune Climb. It's a huge accomplishment if you can climb to the top and look out over Lake Michigan. But it's definitely better tumbling and rolling down after the climb, the wind at your back lifting your shirt like a sail, sand falling into your mouth and every pore. Just be sure you dress comfortably, and take caps, sunscreen, and water.

Stop at the visitor center first to pick up maps, pay your park fee, and see the orientation slide show. Many exhibits there also explain the natural history of the park, and a gift shop sells plush toys, nature books, and kits.

The Pierce Stocking Scenic Drive, located off M-109 south of the Dune Climb and north of the visitor center, is a 7.4-mile car drive through dunes, woods, and breathtaking scenery. Stop often and climb over dunes dotted with foliage. There are many paths to take and overlooks with views of Lake Michigan. Ten suggested stops will only work if your children are patient explorers or if they have had their fill of the real Dune Climb.

Go Box

1157 and 515 East Portage Avenue
(docks 1 & 2)
Sault Ste. Marie 49783

800-432-6301 or 906-632-6301.
www.soolocks.com

Hours vary May–Oct. 15. From June 21
to Aug. 31, boats depart from both docks
Mon.–Sat., from one dock Sun. Check
specific schedule online. Tour is approximately 2 hours.

$19.50 ages 13 & up, $9.50 ages 4–12,
free for children 3 & under

Free on site

10 & up

My Notes

Fun Food

Come to The Antlers Restaurant & Gallery (804 E. Portage Ave., 906-632-3571) for a meal in a noisy restaurant full of stuffed and mounted animals. There are possums, muskrats, calves, skunks, minks, turkeys, bobcats, a cobra, and heads of deer, elk, and bear hung on walls and sitting on platforms. Every so often, horns, whistles, and bells go off to add to the fun. Portions are plentiful, the food is basic and good, and be sure to order root beer. There's a gift shop selling T-shirts, penny candy, and rocks.

Field Tip

Disembark and drive over to the official visitor center (open May–Nov., 800-990-0231) for a historical overview of the Soo Locks, from a movie in the theater to artifacts, photographs, and video displays. You can also walk up to the observation platforms and watch the boats as they chug through the locks.

Soo Locks Boat Tour

Some of the facts learned on the two-hour boat tour are that Sault Ste. Marie is Michigan's oldest city and that there are four locks in the Soo Locks system, responsible for removing or adding 60 gallons of water, which makes the water level go up or down 21 feet.

While it's very exciting being in the boat and experiencing the water gushing in as you go out or receding as you come back, these are the high points of the tour and last only 10 minutes each. If you're on the boat ride with small children, you'll need to amuse them with books, toys, art supplies, and snacks. Bring along hats and sunscreen too. The sun really beats down on the top deck, where you'll want to sit. The horn is fun too. It honks going and coming, but when you least expect it.

Before the boat ride, let the kids have some fun in the building where tickets are sold. The snack bar sells pizza, sandwiches, and ice cream, and the gift shop has a variety of plush animals, puzzles, books, boats, lighthouses, friendship necklaces, Indian tomahawks, dolls, and drums.

125

Go Box

41382 West M-123
Paradise 49768

906-492-3415.
www.michigandnr.com/parksandtrails/Parks
andTrailsInfo.aspx?id=428

Sunup to sundown daily

Free

Daily vehicle pass: $6 resident,
$8 nonresident

All ages

My Notes

Fun Food

Located in the Upper Falls park, Tahquamenon Falls Brewery &
Pub (open year-round except Apr. and Nov., 906-492-3300) is the
best place to eat after a day at the falls. The menu offers variety, the
brew pub has three of its own beers, and the restaurant has air-con-
ditioning. Ask for a root beer or a root beer float. You'll be surprised at how much it looks like the water in the falls. Back in town,
satisfy your craving for soft-serve ice cream at The Scoop (one
block north of the intersection of M-28 and M-123).

Field Tip

If you have children old enough to know how to swim, spend most
of your time in the Lower Falls. Wear swimsuits under your
clothes. Rent a rowboat to take you over to the falls themselves
(this takes less than 10 minutes), and spend half a day frolicking in
the water, walking gingerly from rocky outcrop to rocky outcrop.
The boat fee is $2/person for adults, free for children under 6.

Tahquamenon Falls

Tahquamenon Falls' Upper Falls is one of those awesome natural sites that every Michigander should visit. More than 50,000 gallons of water plummet 50 feet every second over a 200-foot-wide sandstone precipice, making it the second largest falls in the United States east of the Mississippi River, second only to Niagara. While you can hear the gushing water as you get close, you'll need to walk the wooden path and stop at overlooks to see the falls. There are fun descents. Walk down 94 steps at the Brink and 116 steps at the Gorge to see the falls up close. Kids may be surprised to see that the water is the color of root beer. This is caused by tannin from the cedar, spruce, and hemlock trees in the swamps drained by the Tahquamenon River.

With small infants, you are better off using backpack carriers than strollers, so you can more easily take the child with you down steps. Have on hand DEET spray, sunscreen, and caps. Approximately four miles downstream are the Lower Falls, where families can play in the water.

The state park offers naturalist programs from July through Labor Day weekend and seasonal events throughout the year.

CITY INDEX

Northern Michigan and the Upper Peninsula

THEMATIC INDEX